Editorial Project Manager
Lorin E. Klistoff, M.A.

Managing Editor
Karen Goldfluss, M.S. Ed.

Illustrator
Renée Christine Yates

Cover Artist
Tony Carrillo

Art Production Manager
Kevin Barnes

Imaging
James Edward Grace

Publisher
Mary D. Smith, M.S. Ed.

Ages 5-9

Bible Stories & Crafts
Animals

Noah and the Ark
Genesis 6-8

Food for God's People
Exodus 16

God's Wonderful Creation
Genesis 1

Authors
Mary Tucker and Kim Rankin

Teacher Created Resources, Inc.
6421 Industry Way
Westminster, CA 92683
www.teachercreated.com

ISBN: 978-1-4206-7061-5

©2006 Teacher Created Resources, Inc.
Reprinted, 2009
Made in U.S.A.

The classroom teacher may reproduce copies of materials in this book for classroom use only. The reproduction of any part for an entire school or school system is strictly prohibited. No part of this publication may be transmitted, stored, or recorded in any form without written permission from the publisher.

Table of Contents

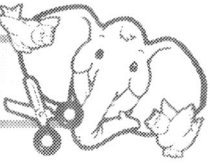

Introduction 4
God's Wonderful Creation 5
Bible Story: Genesis 1 5
Discussion 6
Bible Verse 6
Puppet Skit 6
Crafts: Bookmark, Finger Puppet, Plant Pick,
Handy Clip, and Paper Gift Bag 8
Craft: Animal Door Hanging 12
Craft: Butterfly Growth Wheel 13
A Snake in the Garden 15
Bible Story: Genesis 3 15
Discussion 16
Bible Verse 16
Puppet Skit 16
Craft: Snake Puppet 17
Craft: Doorknob Snake 18
Craft: Spiral Snake Hanger 19
Noah and the Ark 20
Bible Story: Genesis 6–8 20
Discussion 21
Bible Verse 21
Puppet Skit 21
Craft: Animal Stick Puppets 21
Craft: Noah's Ark Mobile 23
Craft: Animal Pencil Holder 25
Craft: Napkin Ring Holders 26
Craft: Bookmark 27
Plagues in Egypt 28
Bible Story: Exodus 7–12 28
Discussion 29
Bible Verse 29
Puppet Skit 29
Craft: Glove Puppets 30
Craft: Hopping Frog 31
Craft: Moving Picture 32
Craft: Locust Model 34
Food for God's People 36
Bible Story: Exodus 16 36
Discussion 36
Bible Verse 36
Puppet Skit 37
Craft: Flying Quail Puppet 37
Craft: Quail Fan 39

Craft: Quail Verse Reminder 40
Ark of the Covenant Comes Home 41
Bible Story: 1 Samuel 4–6 41
Discussion 42
Bible Verse 42
Puppet Skit 42
Craft: Paper Bag Cow Puppet 43
Craft: Moving Picture 44
Craft: Movable Cow 46
Solomon's Riches 47
Bible Story: 1 Kings 10 47
Discussion 47
Bible Verse 48
Puppet Skit 48
Craft: Horse Stick Puppets 49
Craft: 3-D Horse Picture 50
Craft: Horseshoes 52
Solomon Talks About Hard Work 53
Bible Story: Proverbs 6:6–11; 30:24–25 53
Discussion 54
Bible Verse 54
Puppet Skit 54
Craft: Ant Magnet Puppets 55
Craft: Ants Plaque 56
Craft: Picnic Picture 57
Elijah and the Ravens 59
Bible Story: 1 Kings 17:1–6 59
Discussion 60
Bible Verse 60
Puppet Skit 60
Craft: Raven Puppet 61
Craft: Bible Verse Raven 62
Craft: Flying Raven 64
Balaam and His Donkey 66
Bible Story: Numbers 22 66
Discussion 67
Bible Verse 67
Puppet Skit 67
Craft: Donkey Paper Plate Puppet 68
Craft: Donkey Wall Hanging 69
Craft: Donkey Bible Verse Reminder 70
God Talks to Job 72
Bible Story: Job 39:13–18 72
Discussion 73

Table of Contents

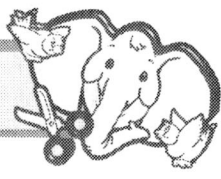

Bible Verse.................... 73
Puppet Skit.................... 73
Craft: Walking Ostrich Puppet............ 74
Craft: Paper Plate Ostrich............... 75
Craft: Ostrich Booklet 77

Daniel and the Lions................. 79
Bible Story: Daniel 6 79
Discussion 80
Bible Verse........................ 80
Puppet Skit........................ 80
Craft: Lion Mask 81
Craft: Lion Refrigerator Magnet 82
Craft: Stand-Up Lion 83

Jonah and the Great Fish............. 85
Bible Story: Jonah 1–2 85
Discussion 86
Bible Verse........................ 86
Puppet Skit........................ 86
Craft: Great Fish Hand Puppet........... 87
Craft: Switch Plate Cover.............. 88
Craft: Jonah Mobile 89

Baby Jesus and Animals.............. 92
Bible Story: Luke 2:1–20; Matthew 2:1–12... 92
Discussion 92
Bible Verse........................ 93
Puppet Skit........................ 93
Craft: Animal Glove Puppets............ 94
Craft: Fingerprint Animals.............. 95
Craft: Camel Pop-Up Card.............. 96

Jesus Is Baptized.................... 99
Bible Story: Matthew 3:13–17;
John 1:29–34 99
Discussion 100
Bible Verse........................ 100
Puppet Skit........................ 100
Craft: Dove Puppet 101
Craft: Baptism Picture 102
Craft: Dove Mobile 104

Jesus Deals with Demons............ 106
Bible Story: Mark 5:1–20.............. 106
Discussion 107
Bible Verse........................ 107
Puppet Skit........................ 107
Craft: Pig Paper Bag Puppet............ 108

Craft: Bible Story Picture Pack 109
Craft: Paper Plate Pig 112

Jesus Talks About Sparrows.......... 114
Bible Story: Matthew 10:28–31 114
Discussion 114
Bible Verse........................ 115
Puppet Skit........................ 115
Craft: Sparrow Head Band 116
Craft: "Jesus Cares" Banner............ 117
Craft: 3-D Tissue Paper Picture 119

The Good Shepherd................. 121
Bible Story: John 10:1–15; Psalm 23...... 121
Discussion 121
Bible Verse........................ 122
Puppet Skit........................ 122
Craft: Sheep Sock Puppet.............. 123
Craft: Lamb Picture Frame............. 124
Craft: Torn-Paper Sheep Picture......... 126

Peter Pays His Taxes 127
Bible Story: Matthew 17:24–27.......... 127
Discussion 127
Bible Verse........................ 128
Puppet Skit........................ 128
Craft: Pipe Cleaner Fish 129
Craft: Fish Picture.................... 130
Craft: Fish Foil Art 132

Jesus Rides into Jerusalem 133
Bible Story: Luke 19:29–40............. 133
Discussion 133
Bible Verse........................ 134
Puppet Skit........................ 134
Craft: Donkey Ears Headband 135
Craft: Donkey Prayer Bag 136
Craft: Service Card Box 137

Peter Denies Jesus.................. 139
Bible Story: Mark 14:30–31, 66–72....... 139
Discussion 139
Bible Verse........................ 140
Puppet Skit........................ 140
Craft: Rooster Stick Puppet 141
Craft: Rooster Magnet 142
Craft: Rooster Clock.................. 143

©Teacher Created Resources #7061 Bible Stories & Crafts: Animals

Introduction

Children love animals and stories about animals. Some very interesting animal stories can be found in the Bible. Many of these stories are not primarily about the animals; in fact, the animals often play a minor part in the story, such as the rooster in the story of Peter's Denial of Jesus. At the same time, the animals are the "co-stars" of some stories, such as Creation, Noah's Ark, Daniel and the Lions, Jonah and the Great Fish, and Balaam and His Donkey. What's both fun and amazing is that God chose so often to use animals to teach important truths to people.

Children, ages 5 through 9, will enjoy and appreciate the stories in this book. They are a cross section of stories from both the Old and New Testaments. Each Bible story is presented in a creative way, using a method that will capture your children's attention and keep it. They include the following: songs to familiar tunes, action rhymes and an echo poem, skits, sketches on the board, the use of easily accessible props, and more. Even the most familiar stories, such as Noah's Ark, will seem new and different and will come alive for children when you use these methods.

Though all the stories are ones regularly included in Sunday School curriculum for kindergarten through elementary school children, some will be more familiar than others.

Each story is followed by discussion questions to help students think about what they've heard and apply its truth to their own lives. A correlated Bible verse is also provided which teachers may want to have children memorize.

Accompanying each Bible story is a puppet skit and directions for making a puppet that children may use to act out the skit. Some of the skits are songs or action rhymes while others are scripts with reading parts for the children and the teacher. The puppets are fun and easy to make, even for younger children.

Each Bible story also includes at least two animal craft ideas. These include the following: bookmarks, a pencil holder, a stand-up horse, plaques, Bible verse reminders, mobiles, pictures with movable parts, a banner, a picture frame, and much more. The crafts have been carefully designed to require easily obtainable items such as card stock, crayons or colored markers, glue, craft sticks, cotton balls, paper plates and bags, foil, yarn, etc. Clear, step-by-step directions are provided for each craft as well as reproducible patterns.

Since each Bible story, skit, and craft stands on its own, they may be plugged into any curriculum or taught one after the other. As your children learn these stories and create the animal crafts, they begin to have a new appreciation for the animals God created and often uses in amazing ways. Even animals can teach us about God's love!

 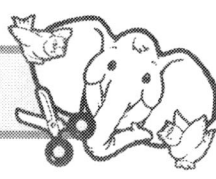

God's Wonderful Creation

Bible Story: Genesis 1

Sing this song with the children.

(*Tune:* "On Top of Old Smokey")

It's hard to imagine how this world began,

So empty and formless, no sky or no land.

Then God spoke a word and everything changed.

All Creation happened just as God arranged.

He made day and night and sky, land, and seas.

Flowers and bushes and all kinds of trees.

Then He created sun, stars, and moon,

Things that would be needed by those coming soon.

The very next day He created the birds,

All singing and squawking like you've never heard—

Bluebirds and robins and doves in the sky,

Ostrich and penguins who weren't made to fly.

Then he made fish and sea creatures galore

To swim and to crawl on the deep ocean floor—

Catfish and sharks and tuna and whales,

Starfish and shrimp and oysters and snails.

Next God made creatures to live on the land—

Monkeys and hippos and lions and lambs,

Horses and squirrels and big kangaroos,

Rabbits and rhinos and elephants too.

Then God made man as only He could,

And everything God created was good!

After all that, the man played a game,

Giving each animal just the right name.

©Teacher Created Resources #7061 Bible Stories & Crafts: Animals

 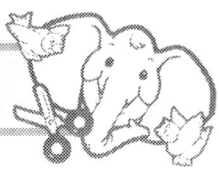

God's Wonderful Creation

Discussion

- Why do you think God created the sun, sea, sky, land, and plants before He created birds, fish, and animals?
- God created many thousands of different kinds of animals. What is your favorite animal? Why?
- How do animals benefit us? Why do we need them?

Bible Verse

"How many are your works, O LORD! In wisdom you made them all; the earth is full of your creatures." (Psalm 104:24)

What do animals teach us about God?

Puppet Skit

Follow the directions on page 8 to make finger puppets. Then have children use the puppets to act out the following skit. Choose one child to be Adam and six children to be the animals. Point out that God did not give the animals He created the ability to speak, so when the animals speak in this skit, it is only what they are thinking in their heads. Adam does not hear them.

Adam: Thank You, God, for creating all these wonderful animals. Now You want me to give a name to each one. Well, let me see, I will have to think carefully. Hello, little bug. You are a cute thing. I think I will call you a ladybug.

Ladybug: Ladybug! I am not a lady; I am a boy! Come on, try again, Adam. You can come up with a better name than that, can't you? God created me such a bright red color with these nice black spots. How about calling me the Red Beast or something impressive like that? I may be little, but God had a reason for creating me.

Adam: Yes, from now on you will be known as the ladybug. *(Turn to the bear.)* Well, you are a big guy! What should I call you?

Bear: I love to eat almost anything, but especially bugs. How about naming me after food? And God created me big and strong with sharp claws and teeth. Maybe I should have a scary name. Whatever you call me, God says creating me was a good idea.

Adam: I'm going to call you Bear. I don't know why; the name just seems to fit you!

Cat: Meow! Meow!

Adam: You are a friendly animal and I like your whiskers. Hmm, I am going to give you a very simple name. How about Cat? Do you like that name?

Cat: Purrr, purrr. I think it is purrr-fect.

Adam: My goodness! You are so small I almost didn't see you down there. I see that you are very quick too. I need to think of a good name for you.

#7061 Bible Stories & Crafts: Animals ©Teacher Created Resources

 # God's Wonderful Creation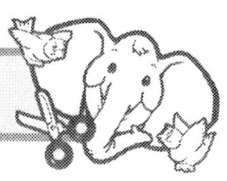

Puppet Skit *(cont.)*

Mouse: Squeak! Squeak! I may be small, but the Creator made me with special care. Hurry up and think of a name so I can run back in my hole! I don't like the way that cat is looking at me.

Adam: How about Mouse? Yes, I think that suits you. Now off you go!

Wolf: Howwwl! Howwwl!

Adam: Hello there. God created a strong, fierce animal when He made you! You need a strong, fierce name. I will call you Wolf.

Wolf: I love to run through the woods and howl in the moonlight. Wolf is a good name for me.

Adam: You have nice, soft fur, and God gave you such big ears. You must hear better than anybody! I think you would make a nice pet.

Rabbit: The Creator gave me big back feet so I can hop and run fast. I am glad that He made plants before He made me because there is a big patch of clover over there that I am going to go nibble on as soon as I have a name.

Adam: I am going to call you Rabbit. It is an excellent name for an excellent animal!

Animals: (All animals make their special sounds or run or jump around happily.)

Adam: Thank You, God, for these animals and all the other animals You created. You are so great and everything You created is very good.

©Teacher Created Resources #7061 Bible Stories & Crafts: Animals

God's Wonderful Creation
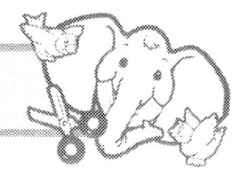

Crafts: Bookmark, Finger Puppet, Plant Pick, Handy Clip, and Paper Gift Bag

Materials

- patterns on page 9–11
- crayons, markers, or colored pencils
- clear adhesive plastic
- craft sticks for bookmarks
- cardstock or poster board
- stapler and staples
- scissors
- tape or glue
- curling ribbon
- clothespins for clips
- magnets
- lunch bags
- 6" to 8" wooden dowel rods or wood stakes for plant picks

Bookmark

Directions

1. Copy the patterns onto cardstock or poster board.
2. Color the patterns.
3. Cover the patterns with clear adhesive plastic and then cut them out.
4. Make one of the following crafts:

   Bookmark: Tape or glue an animal pattern to a craft stick. Write a Bible verse or message on the craft stick and give it to a special person.
   Finger Puppet: Use the finger puppet patterns on page 9. Make as many copies as needed. Glue or staple an animal pattern from pages 10 and 11 to the finger puppet pattern. Then glue or staple the ends together. Now your puppet is ready for a finger play or story.
   Plant Pick: Tape or glue an animal pattern to the top of a dowel rod or wooden stake.
   Handy Clip: Tape or glue an animal pattern to a clothespin. Use the clip on a chip or cereal bag. Glue a magnet to the back to put on the refrigerator.
   Paper Gift Bag: Copy several animal patterns and color them. Glue them on a paper lunch bag. Fold the bag two inches over and use a hole punch to punch two holes. Loop curling ribbon through the holes and tie a bow.

Finger Puppets

Paper Gift Bag

Plant Pick

Handy Clip

#7061 Bible Stories & Crafts: Animals ©Teacher Created Resources

 # God's Wonderful Creation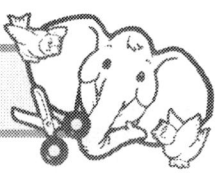

Crafts: Bookmark, Finger Puppet, Plant Pick, Handy Clip, and Paper Gift Bag *(cont.)*

Finger Puppet Patterns

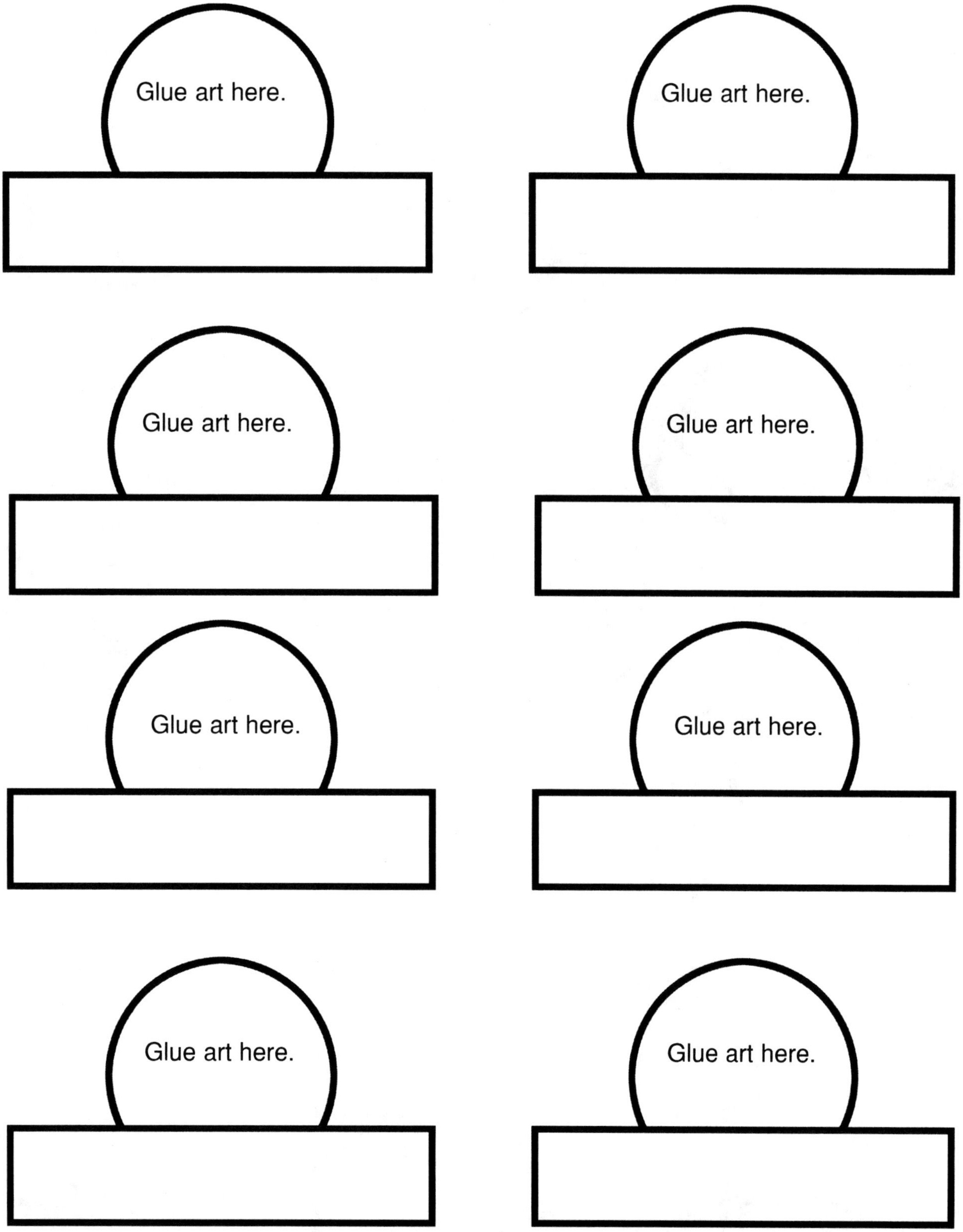

Glue art here.

Glue art here.

Glue art here.

Glue art here.

Glue art here.

Glue art here.

Glue art here.

Glue art here.

©Teacher Created Resources #7061 Bible Stories & Crafts: Animals

God's Wonderful Creation

Crafts: Bookmark, Finger Puppet, Plant Pick, Handy Clip, and Paper Gift Bag *(cont.)*

Animal Patterns

God's Wonderful Creation

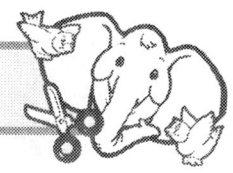

Crafts: Bookmark, Finger Puppet, Plant Pick, Handy Clip, and Paper Gift Bag *(cont.)*
Animal Patterns

God's Wonderful Creation

Craft: Animal Door Hanging

Materials

- pattern below
- glue
- clear adhesive plastic
- cardstock or poster board
- crayons, markers, or colored pencils
- scissors
- hole punch
- 12" chenille sticks

Directions

1. Copy the pattern onto white cardstock or poster board.
2. Color the pattern.
3. Cover the pattern with clear adhesive plastic and cut it out. Punch holes in the dark circles.
4. Use the chenille stick to connect the sign and the elephant pattern. Add another chenille stick to make the loop at the top to hang.
5. Glue the bird onto the elephant.

Finished Product

Let every creature, large and small, Praise the Lord who made them all!

#7061 Bible Stories & Crafts: Animals — ©Teacher Created Resources

 # God's Wonderful Creation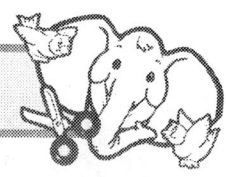

Craft: Butterfly Growth Wheel

Materials
- patterns on pages 13 and 14
- white cardstock
- scissors
- brad fasteners
- crayons, markers, or colored pencils

Finished Product

Directions
1. Copy the patterns onto white cardstock.
2. Color and cut out the patterns.
3. Insert a brass fastener into the center dot of pattern A. Then insert the brass fastener into the center dot of pattern B. Bend the back of the fastener to hold the two circles together.
4. Turn the wheel to show the life cycle of a butterfly. Discuss how God not only created butterflies, but also carefully planned how they would be born and develop.

Pattern A

©Teacher Created Resources   13   #7061 Bible Stories & Crafts: Animals

 # God's Wonderful Creation

Craft: Butterfly Growth Wheel *(cont.)*

Pattern B

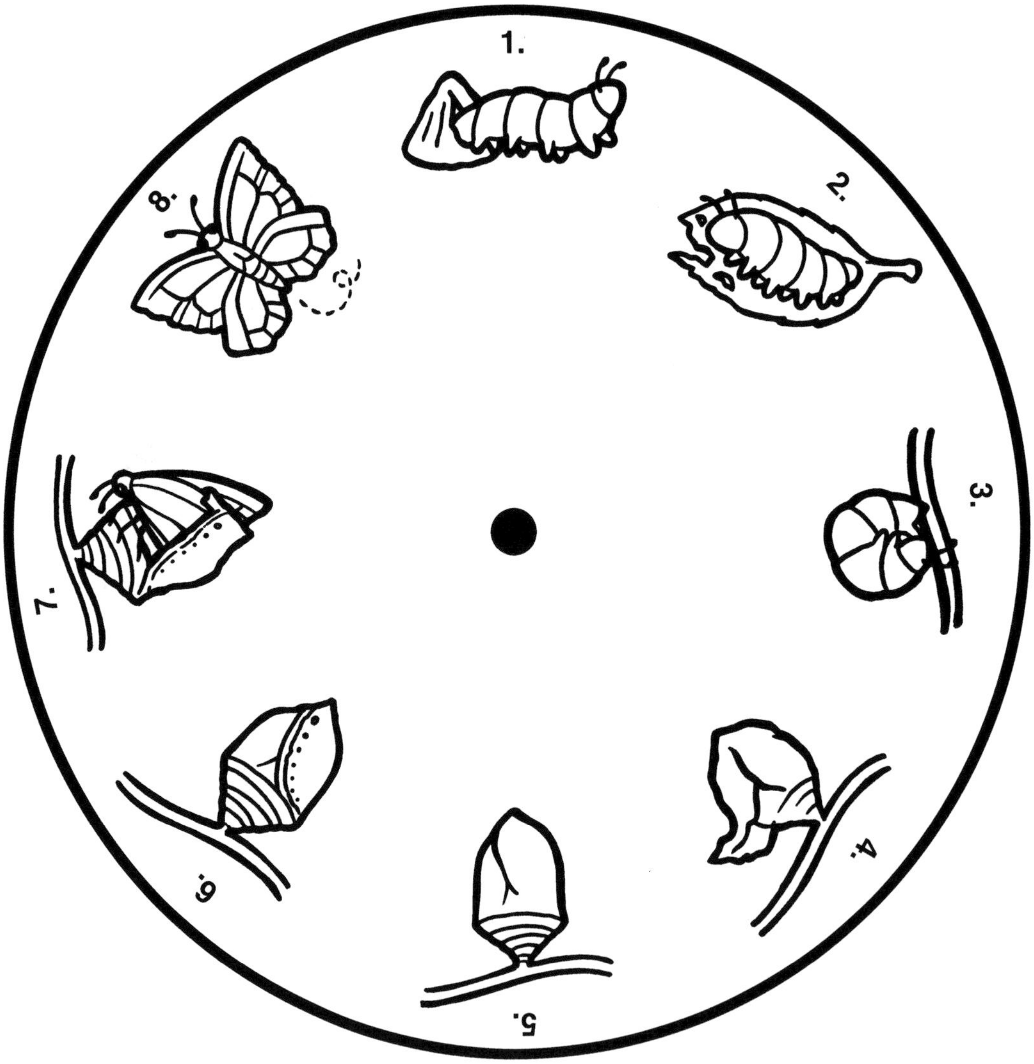

#7061 Bible Stories & Crafts: Animals ©Teacher Created Resources

 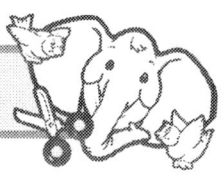

A Snake in the Garden

Bible Story: Genesis 3

As you tell the Bible story, use your hand and arm to represent the serpent. Move your arm in an undulating motion and hold your hand slightly cupped with the fingers and thumb close together for the snake's head. Practice in front of a mirror to perfect the movements before you do it for your students.

After God created the man, He named Him Adam. Then He created a woman and called her Eve. Adam and Eve were perfect and lived in the perfect Garden of Eden. They did not have to work hard; God gave them everything they could possibly want. The quiet garden was never disturbed with the noise of anger or arguing. Even the animals all got along together. But God created Adam and Eve with a free will, and it was not long before they chose to do wrong.

God gave the man and woman just one rule to follow. "You are free to eat from any tree in the garden," God told Adam, "except the tree of knowledge of good and evil. You must not eat the fruit from that tree. If you do, you will die." Adam and Eve probably both thought, "That is no problem. We would never disobey God. We want to do what He tells us." But soon their attitudes changed.

Living in that beautiful garden was a serpent, more clever than all the other animals God had created. *(Move your arm like the serpent until its "face" is toward the children.)* One day the serpent spoke to Eve. "Did God really say you must not eat from any tree in the garden?" it asked. Eve explained that they had permission to eat from any of the trees except one, the tree of knowledge of good and evil. She added that they were not allowed to even touch it, though God never said that.

"You won't die," the serpent told Eve. *(Shake the serpent's head "no.")* "God knows that if you eat from that tree, your eyes will be opened and you will be like Him! You will know good and evil."

Sadly, Eve listened to the serpent and accepted what it said. Instead of trusting God she began to doubt, and she began to want a taste of that mysterious fruit. It looked good and the serpent said it would make her wise. She picked a piece of fruit of that forbidden tree and took a bite of it. *(Pretend to hold fruit in one hand and bite it as your "serpent" hand watches and shakes its head "yes.")*

But Eve did not disobey God all alone; she gave some of the fruit to Adam too. Adam should have refused to eat the fruit, but he disobeyed God just as Eve had. As soon as he ate the fruit, he and Eve were changed. They hadn't worn clothes before and were not embarrassed about it. But suddenly, Adam and Eve felt the need to cover their bodies. They made clothes from fig leaves and put them on. Then they hid from God. They were afraid of Him because of their disobedience. Of course, no one can hide from God. He sees and knows everything.

God punished Adam and Eve and made them leave the beautiful garden. He even stationed angels with a sword at the entrance so they could not sneak back in. God also punished the serpent for tempting the man and woman to sin. "You will crawl on your belly and you will eat dust all the days of your life," God told it. Since then, snakes have had to crawl to get where they want to go. *(Move the snake back and forth.)*

Many people do not like snakes or are afraid of them. The serpent in the Garden of Eden was actually the devil disguised as a snake. The snakes we see today are just animals God created. We need to stay away from them, especially those that are poisonous, but they cannot tempt us to do wrong. Only the devil can do that. God helps us obey Him and fight against the temptations of the devil.

©Teacher Created Resources   #7061 Bible Stories & Crafts: Animals

A Snake in the Garden

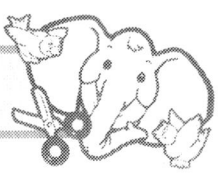

Discussion

- Why do you think Eve listened to the serpent?
- Why is it easier to give in to the temptation to do wrong than to fight it?
- How does God help you not give in?

Bible Verse

Jesus said, "I am sending you out like sheep among wolves. Therefore be as shrewd as snakes and as innocent as doves." (Matthew 10:16)

"Shrewd" means *clever or smart*. Jesus was speaking of snakes in a good way, encouraging his disciples to be as clever as snakes are. Of course, He was talking about regular snakes, not the devil disguised as a snake. How do you think snakes show that they are clever?

Puppet Skit

Follow the directions on page 17 to make snake puppets. Then have children use the puppets to act out the following rhyming monologue skit.

> I am a snake, a special kind,
> For Satan used me to change Eve's mind.
> She wanted to do whatever God said,
> But when I spoke she believed me instead.
> I told her a lie and she believed.
> She disobeyed God and He was grieved.
> Then she went and got Adam to sin.
> That made me so happy I had to grin.
> Sin entered the Garden of Eden that day
> And when they heard God, the two hid away.
> God punished them and He punished me too,
> Now I have to slither, not walk like you.
> Of course, it wasn't the fault of the snake.
> It was Adam and Eve who made the mistake.
> Snakes are just animals, skinny and long.
> It was Satan who tempted Eve to do wrong.

#7061 Bible Stories & Crafts: Animals — ©Teacher Created Resources

 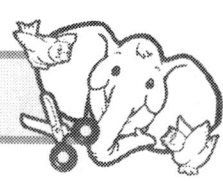

A Snake in the Garden

Craft: Snake Puppet

Materials
- tube sock
- red marker
- red fabric
- buttons or craft wiggly eyes
- glue
- scissors

Finished Product

Directions

1. Put the tube sock on your hand. Push in the center part of the sock and use your thumb and fingers to make a mouth. Use the red marker to mark the center of the mouth where you will glue the snake's tongue.

2. Take the sock off your hand. Trace around the tongue pattern on red fabric and cut it out.

3. Glue the fabric tongue to the sock where you put the red mark.

4. Glue two buttons or craft eyes on the sock above the mouth.

5. Let the glue dry thoroughly. Then put the sock on your hand and move your thumb and fingers to make the snake puppet talk.

6. Move your hand and arm in a spiraling motion to make the puppet move like a snake.

7. Use your snake puppet to do the skit on page 16.

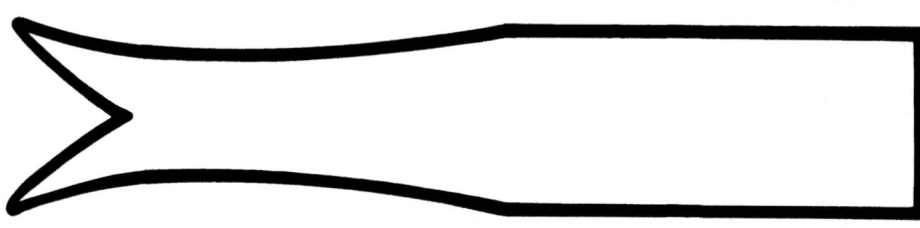

Tongue Pattern

©Teacher Created Resources 17 #7061 Bible Stories & Crafts: Animals

A Snake in the Garden

Craft: Doorknob Snake

Materials

- pattern on this page
- scissors
- cardstock or poster board
- crayons, markers, or colored pencils
- clear adhesive plastic

Directions

1. Copy the pattern onto cardstock or poster board.
2. Color the pattern.
3. Cover the pattern with clear adhesive plastic.
4. Cut it out and hang it on your doorknob to remind you not to sin.

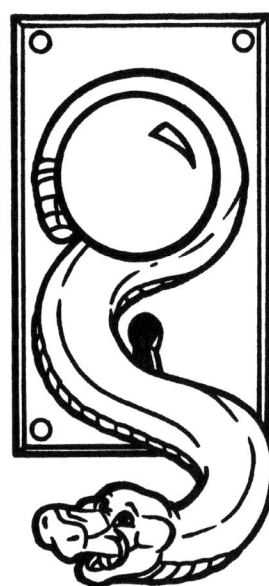

Finished Product

#7061 Bible Stories & Crafts: Animals ©Teacher Created Resources

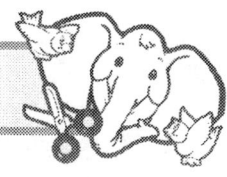

A Snake in the Garden

Craft: Spiral Snake Hanger

Materials

- scissors
- yarn or string
- hole punch
- stapler
- snake pattern and verse card on this page
- colored cardstock or poster board

> The wages of sin is death, but the gift of God is eternal life. (Romans 6:23a)

Directions

1. Copy the Bible verse card and snake pattern onto colored cardstock or poster board.
2. Cut out the spiral on the snake pattern.
3. Punch a hole through the end of the snake's tail.
4. Use a 4–6 inch piece of string or yarn to hang the snake from its tail.
5. Cut out the Bible verse card. Staple the card to the yarn or string as shown below.

Finished Product

©Teacher Created Resources   #7061 Bible Stories & Crafts: Animals

Noah and the Ark

Bible Story: Genesis 6-8

As you tell the Bible story, have children make the repetitive sounds and movements with you as noted.

People on the earth were so wicked God decided to destroy almost everybody and everything in a great flood. He chose a man named Noah to build a huge boat that would be the means of saving some people and animals so the earth could start again once the flood was over. Noah immediately obeyed God and began building the boat. Pound! Pound! Pound! *(Knock on table with knuckles.)* Noah hammered the boards into place. It was hard work, but Noah kept at it month after month until finally the big boat was done.

Then it was time to obey the rest of God's directions and start loading the boat with people and animals. God brought all the animals to Noah. Clop! Clop! Clop! Clop! *(Make clopping noises with tongue.)* Horses and zebras and deer climbed into the boat. Thud! Thud! Thud! *(Stamp feet on floor.)* The big elephants walked into the boat. Growl! Growl! *(Make growling noises.)* The lions and tigers, bears and wolves went into the boat. Big animals and little animals, alligators and anteaters, koalas and kangeroos, hippos and hyenas all went into the boat and settled down.

Noah and his sons had already loaded the boat with plenty of food for the animals and people. Then Noah's wife, his four sons, and their wives went into the boat. Thud! *(Smack table with hand.)* God Himself shut the door, and the rain began. Drip, drop! Drip, drop! *(Make dripping noises.)* The rain fell on the ground and soon puddles were everywhere. It kept raining and raining for 40 days and nights until everything on the earth was covered with water, even the mountains. As far as you could see there was nothing but water and Noah's big boat floating on it. All living, breathing things on the earth were destroyed. But those on the boat were safe and dry.

Back and forth, back and forth the big boat swayed as the waves pushed it around. *(Sway back and forth.)* Finally, the rain stopped. The earth was silent except for the sound of the water slapping against the sides of the boat. But how noisy it must have been inside the ark with people talking and laughing and animals howling, growling, trumpeting, quacking, barking, squeaking and squawking! *(Let children make the noises of their favorite animals.)*

For a whole year Noah's family and the animals lived on the boat. Then one day Noah opened a window and released a raven, a big blackbird. Flap, flap! Flap, flap! *(Flap arms slowly.)* The big bird was a strong flyer and it kept flying over the flooded earth until it found a place dry enough to land. A little later Noah released a dove from the window. Flap, flap, flap! Flap, flap, flap! *(Flap arms quickly.)* The dove was not as strong as the raven and was not able to fly as far or as long. It flew back to Noah in the ark when it could not find a dry place to land. A week later Noah sent the dove out again and it returned with a green leaf in its beak. That showed Noah that the water had gone down enough for some trees to be above water. A week later Noah sent the dove out again and this time it did not return. Noah knew if the dove had found a place to stay the water had gone down much more. Before long the water was gone and the earth was dry. The big boat had come to rest on a mountain and God told Noah it was time to leave the ark. Thumpity, thump! Clumpity, clump! Clop, clop, clop! *(Make noises of animals running with your feet and tongue.)* The animals hurried off the boat, quickly followed by Noah and his family. It was time to start over, to make new homes, and have babies to repopulate the earth.

Noah made an offering to God, thanking Him for keeping them all safe. Then God put a beautiful rainbow in the sky as a reminder of His promise to never again destroy the earth with a flood.

Noah and the Ark

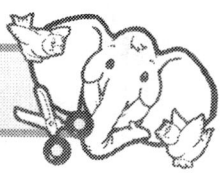

Discussion

- Why did God send Noah two of each animal to go on the ark?
- How would our lives be different today if all the animals on earth had died in the flood?
- Why should we be thankful for animals?

Bible Verse

"For every animal of the forest is mine, and the cattle on a thousand hills." (Psalm 50:10)

Who made the animals? How does He care for them?

Puppet Skit

Follow the directions below to make the stick puppets. Then have students use them to act out this rhyming skit. Choose one student to read the part of Noah. All the other students will be the animals.

Noah: The boat is ready and today's the day. Come aboard, everyone, without delay!

Monkeys: Chee, chee, chee! Happy monkeys are we. We will do what you say if you'll let us play.

Elephants: So this is the place. Is there plenty of space? We are so big, you know, we must watch where we go.

Lions: Look out, all of you! We are ferocious, it is true. But we will try to be good because we know we should.

Giraffes: Is there room for our necks, maybe up on top deck? God made us so tall, everything else seems small.

Dogs: Arf! Arf! Come on, let's chase the cats in this place!

Cats: Meow! Meow! Leave us alone. We just want to sleep and be on our own.

Owls: Hoo—Hoo! We are coming aboard, where we know we will be safe in the hands of the Lord.

Noah: You are right, that is for sure. God has said we will endure. Through the lightning and storm, we will be safe, dry, and warm in God's special boat that He promised will float! All aboard!

Craft: Animal Stick Puppets

Materials

- animal patterns on page 22
- craft sticks or tongue depressors
- colored pencils or markers
- heavy cardstock paper
- glue
- scissors

Directions

1. Copy the animal patterns on page 22 onto heavy cardstock paper and divide them among students to color and cut out.
2. Provide each student with a craft stick or tongue depressor and glue. Have them glue a craft stick or tongue depressor on each animal pattern.
3. They may hold up the puppets to act out the rhyming skit above.

©Teacher Created Resources   #7061 Bible Stories & Crafts: Animals

Noah and the Ark

Craft: Animal Stick Puppets *(cont.)*

Follow the directions on page 21.

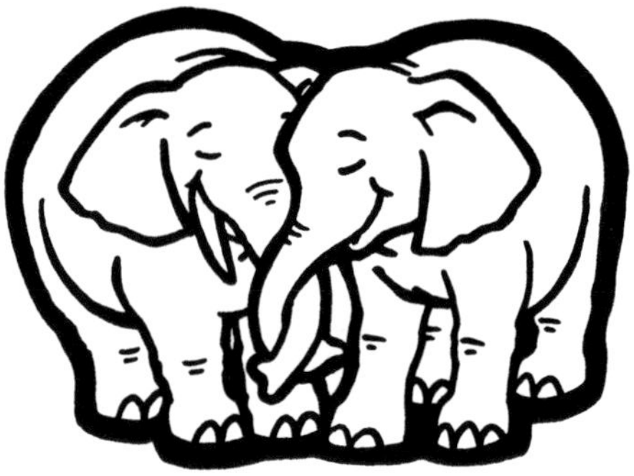

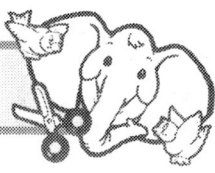

Noah and the Ark

Craft: Noah's Ark Mobile

Materials

- patterns on pages 23–24
- cardstock paper or poster board
- crayons, markers, or colored pencils
- yarn or string
- scissors
- glue
- hole punch

Finished Product

Directions

1. Copy the patterns onto cardstock or poster board.
2. Color the patterns and cut them out.
3. Glue the rainbow to the backside of the ark as shown.
4. Glue the sun in place on the rainbow.
5. Punch holes where indicated and tie various lengths of yarn. Attach the animals to the yarn.
6. Tie 15" piece of string to the top piece for a hanger.

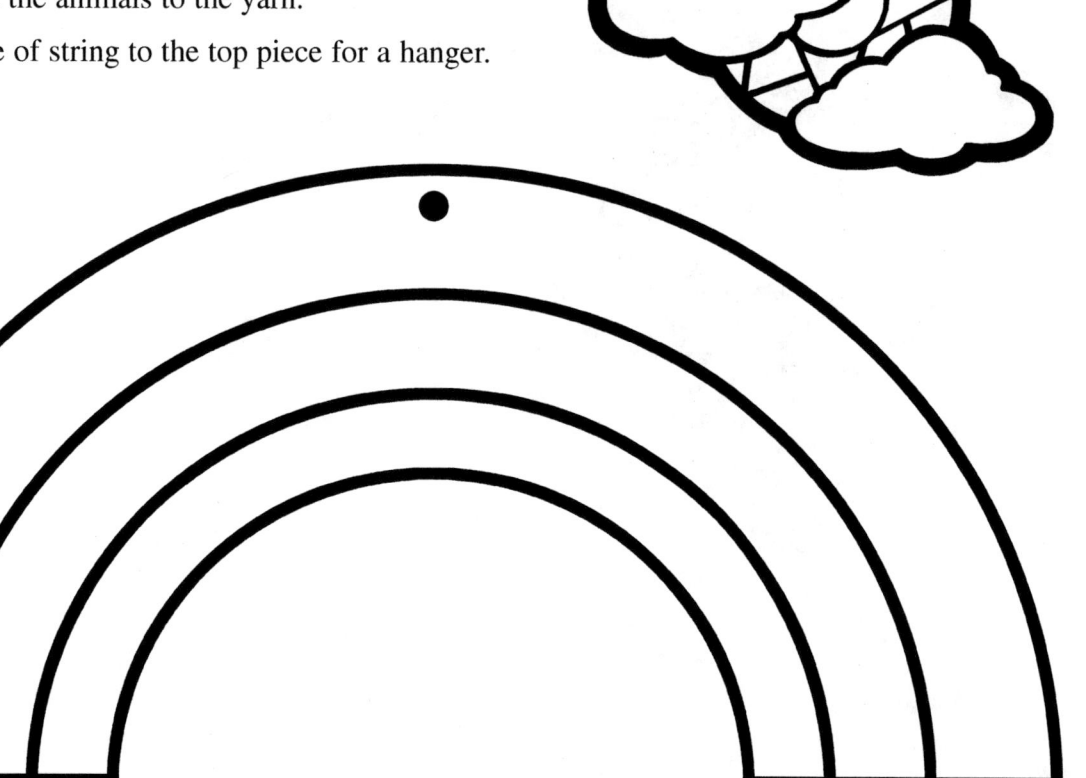

©Teacher Created Resources 23 #7061 Bible Stories & Crafts: Animals

Noah and the Ark

Craft: Noah's Ark Mobile *(cont.)*

See page 23 for directions.

#7061 Bible Stories & Crafts: Animals ©Teacher Created Resources

Noah and the Ark

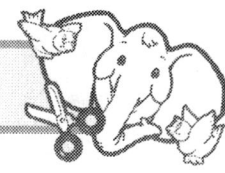

Craft: Animal Pencil Holder

Materials

- white paper
- pattern below
- tape
- scissors
- crayons, markers, or colored pencils
- clear adhesive plastic
- tin can or a small, cylinder chip or soup container
- colored construction paper *(optional)*

Directions

1. Copy the pattern onto white paper.
2. Color the pattern.
3. Cover the pattern with clear adhesive plastic.
4. Cut the pattern out, wrap it around the can, and tape it. (*Optional:* You may wish to cover the can first with colored construction paper to cover any excess areas that the pattern does not cover.)
5. Place pencils or pens in the can.

Finished Product

©Teacher Created Resources   25   #7061 *Bible Stories & Crafts: Animals*

 # Noah and the Ark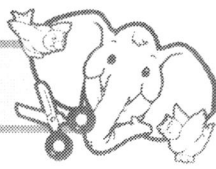

Craft: Napkin Ring Holders

Materials

- patterns below
- cardstock or poster board
- crayons, markers, or colored pencils
- glue or tape
- scissors
- napkins

Finished Product

Directions

1. Copy the patterns onto cardstock or poster board.
2. Color and cut out the patterns.
3. Fold the triangle at the bottom, then pull the top of the triangles up and tape them as shown in the picture to the right.
4. Cut out the ark pattern. Tape or glue the center of the ark to the triangular shape napkin holder.
5. Place napkin inside the triangle and place it on the table.

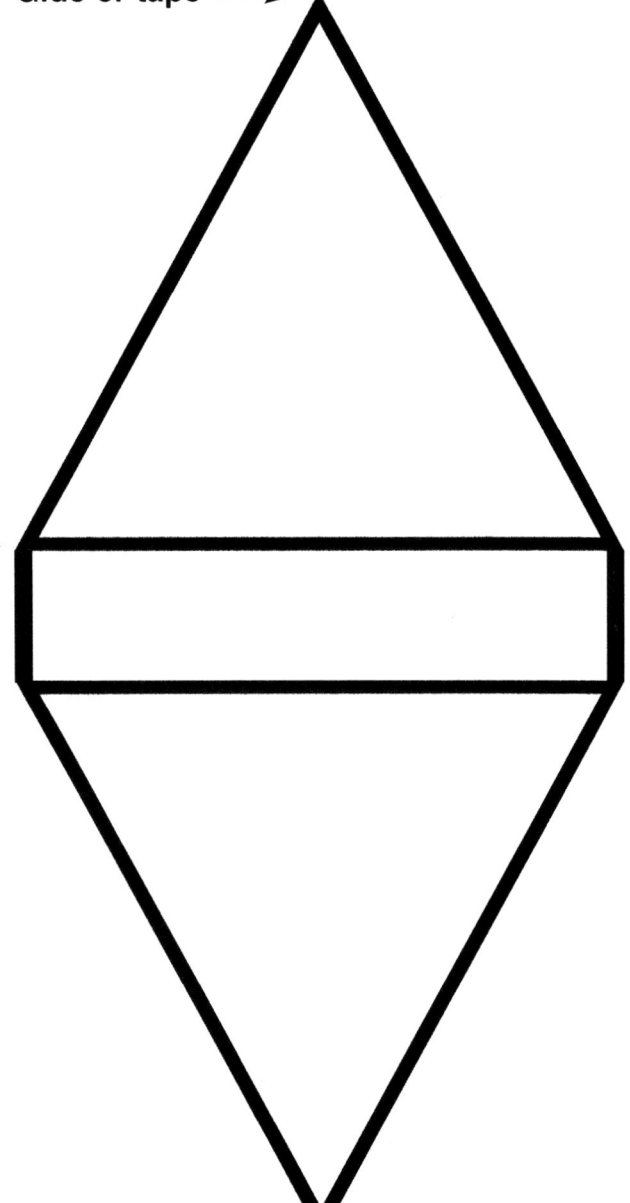

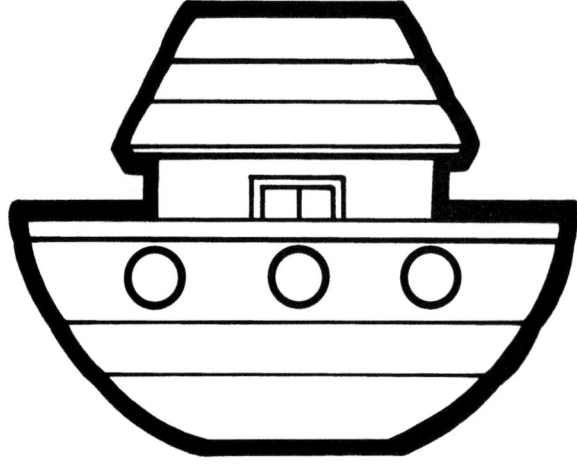

#7061 Bible Stories & Crafts: Animals   26   ©Teacher Created Resources

Noah and the Ark
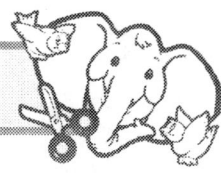

Craft: Bookmark

Materials

- pattern below
- white paper
- clear adhesive plastic
- crayons, markers, or colored pencils
- wide ribbon or fabric (about 3" wide)
- scissors
- glue

Directions

1. Copy the pattern onto white paper.
2. Color the pattern.
3. Cover the bookmark with clear adhesive plastic to protect it.
4. Then cut out the pattern.
5. Glue the pattern to a piece of ribbon or fabric, about 3" x 6".

Finished Product

 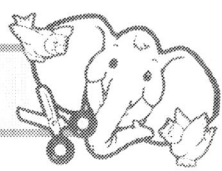

Plagues in Egypt

Bible Story: Exodus 7-12

As you tell about the encounters between Moses and Pharaoh, hold up a paper plate on which you have drawn an angry face (Pharaoh) and one with a calm face on it (Moses).

God wanted His people out of Egypt. He sent Moses to talk to Pharaoh, the king, but Pharaoh would not listen. God decided to afflict the Egyptian people with plagues until Pharaoh changed his mind.

Moses went to the river to talk to Pharaoh (*hold up calm face*). He told Pharaoh that God wanted him to let His people go. Pharaoh refused (*hold up angry face*). "This is what the Lord says," Moses replied (*hold up calm face*), "'By this you will know that I am the Lord.'" Then he struck the river with his staff. Immediately, the water turned into blood. The fish in the river died and no one could drink its water. But Pharaoh did not change his mind.

A week later Moses went to see Pharaoh again (*hold up calm face*). "If you do not do what the Lord says, He will cause frogs to cover the land." Pharaoh would not listen (*hold up angry face*) so God brought frogs everywhere—on the roads, in the houses, even in people's beds! But Pharaoh (*hold up angry face*) refused to let God's people go.

Next, God brought gnats to plague the people. They were everywhere, crawling on the people and their animals and biting them. But Pharaoh (*hold up angry face*) was too stubborn to give in.

Moses told Pharaoh (*hold up calm face*), "God has said He will send swarms of flies on Egypt unless you agree to let His people go." Once again (*hold up angry face*), Pharaoh said no. The next day flies covered people's arms and legs and faces and got into everything. But there were no flies in the homes of God's people. Still, Pharaoh (*hold up angry face*) would not obey God.

Moses warned Pharaoh (*hold up calm face*) that if he did not give in, the livestock (horses, donkeys, camels, sheep, and goats) would die. Pharaoh (*hold up angry face*) scowled at Moses and refused. The next day the Egyptians' animals got sick and died, but those belonging to the Israelites were fine.

God told Moses to throw some soot from a furnace into the air. When he did, painful boils broke out on the bodies of the Egyptian people, but not the Israelites. Pharaoh's magicians could not come to him because they were so sick from the boils. But Pharaoh (*hold up angry face*) did not change his mind.

Moses went to see Pharaoh again (*hold up calm face*). He told the king that God could have wiped the Egyptians off the earth, but instead He was showing them His power. Pharaoh needed to pay attention and do what God asked or He would send the worst hailstorm Egypt had ever seen. Moses warned Pharaoh to have people put their animals in barns and stay in shelter themselves because the hail would kill anyone outside. Pharaoh did not listen (*hold up angry face*), but some of his people did. When the hail fell, only those who were under shelter were saved. All animals and people out in the open were killed, except for the Israelites. There was no hail where they were.

Moses told Pharaoh (*hold up calm face*) God would send locusts to eat the remaining plants and crops if Pharaoh did not let His people go. Pharaoh (*hold up angry face*) refused. The next day locusts covered the ground, eating every plant. No green thing was left, except where the Israelites lived.

God told Moses to stretch out his hand and darkness came over the land of Egypt for three days. Yet, all the Israelites had light where they lived. Pharaoh (*hold up angry face*) would still not listen to God.

#7061 Bible Stories & Crafts: Animals ©Teacher Created Resources

Plagues in Egypt

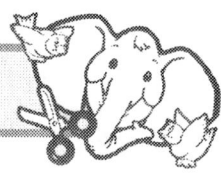

Bible Story: Exodus 7–12 *(cont.)*

One last time Moses went to warn Pharaoh (*hold up calm face*). He said to Pharaoh, "God is going to bring death to the land. If you do not let my people go, every firstborn son in every Egyptian family will die. Even the firstborn animals will die." Only those who obeyed God's instructions would survive. But Pharaoh would not give in (*hold up angry face*). One night the Lord kept His promise and struck down every firstborn son—even Pharaoh's son. Finally, Pharaoh was ready to listen (*hold up angry face*). Pharaoh told Moses to take his people and get out of the land. Moses did not waste any time. He quickly began to lead God's people out of Egypt. God had rescued them from slavery just as He promised.

Discussion

- How did God show kindness to His people throughout the plagues?
- How did He show kindness to the Egyptian people?
- How did the plagues show God's great power?

Bible Verse

"Who can proclaim the mighty acts of the LORD or fully declare his praise?" (Psalm 106:2)
What are some "mighty acts" God has done in your life?

Puppet Skit

Follow the directions on page 30 to make glove puppets. Have children use their puppets to act out this rhyming skit. They should hold up the fingers with the appropriate animals as they are mentioned.

Terrible plagues hit Egypt land sent directly by God's hand.

A river of blood and painful sores, hail and darkness, and even more!

God used animals and insects too, to make Pharaoh do what he should do.

He sent a lot of frogs one day to be everywhere and in everyone's way.

Then God sent gnats to buzz and bite people and animals all day and night.

After that came swarms of flies—crawling in people's ears and eyes.

Then people's animals started to die. They just fell down dead, no one knew why!

Locusts came like you've never seen, and ate every single thing that was green.

Finally, Pharaoh gave in with a cry when God caused his firstborn son to die.

 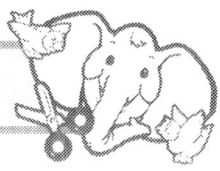

Plagues in Egypt

Craft: Glove Puppets

Materials

- patterns below
- cardstock
- crayons, markers, or colored pencils
- children's gloves (Have children bring old ones from home.)
- craft glue
- scissors

Directions

1. Copy the five patterns onto cardstock.
2. Have children color them.
3. Help each child trace a hand, fingers slightly separated, on cardstock and cut it out.
4. Cut out the patterns and carefully glue one pattern to each finger (and thumb) of the glove. In order to keep the glue from soaking through the gloves and sticking the fingers together, insert the cardstock hand shape into the glove before gluing the patterns on the fingers.
5. Let the glue dry completely.
6. Then have children carefully put their gloves on and wiggle their fingers to make the puppets move.

Finished Product

#7061 Bible Stories & Crafts: Animals ©Teacher Created Resources

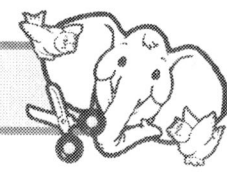

Plagues in Egypt

Craft: Hopping Frog

Materials

- patterns below
- string
- cardstock or poster board
- crayons, markers, or colored pencils
- glue
- hole punch
- scissors

Directions

1. Copy the patterns onto cardstock or poster board.
2. Color the patterns and cut them out.
3. Accordion fold the frog's legs.
4. Glue the folded legs to the small rectangles near the bottom of the frog.
5. Punch a small hole in the top of the frog with a hole punch.
6. Attach string to the frog.
7. Hop the frog along the floor on his long folded legs.

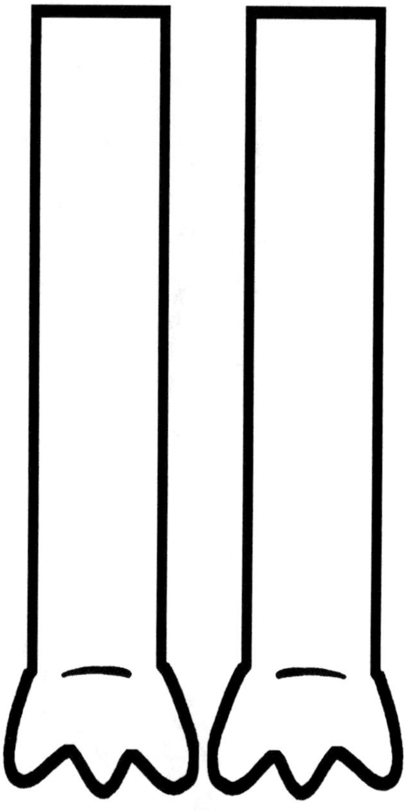

Finished Product

©Teacher Created Resources 31 #7061 Bible Stories & Crafts: Animals

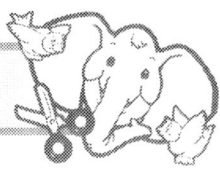

Plagues in Egypt

Craft: Moving Picture

Materials

- patterns below
- picture on page 33
- cardstock or poster board
- crayons, markers, or colored pencils
- scissors and glue stick
- brad fasteners
- glitter or glitter glue

Finished Product

Directions

1. Copy the patterns and the picture onto cardstock or poster board.
2. Color the patterns and the picture.
3. Cut out the arm patterns.
4. Use brad fasteners to attach the arms to the people and the tail to the cow in the picture.
5. Spread glue over much of the picture, and sprinkle glitter on the glue to represent gnats and flies.
6. Let the people move their arms and the cow move its tail to chase away the insects.

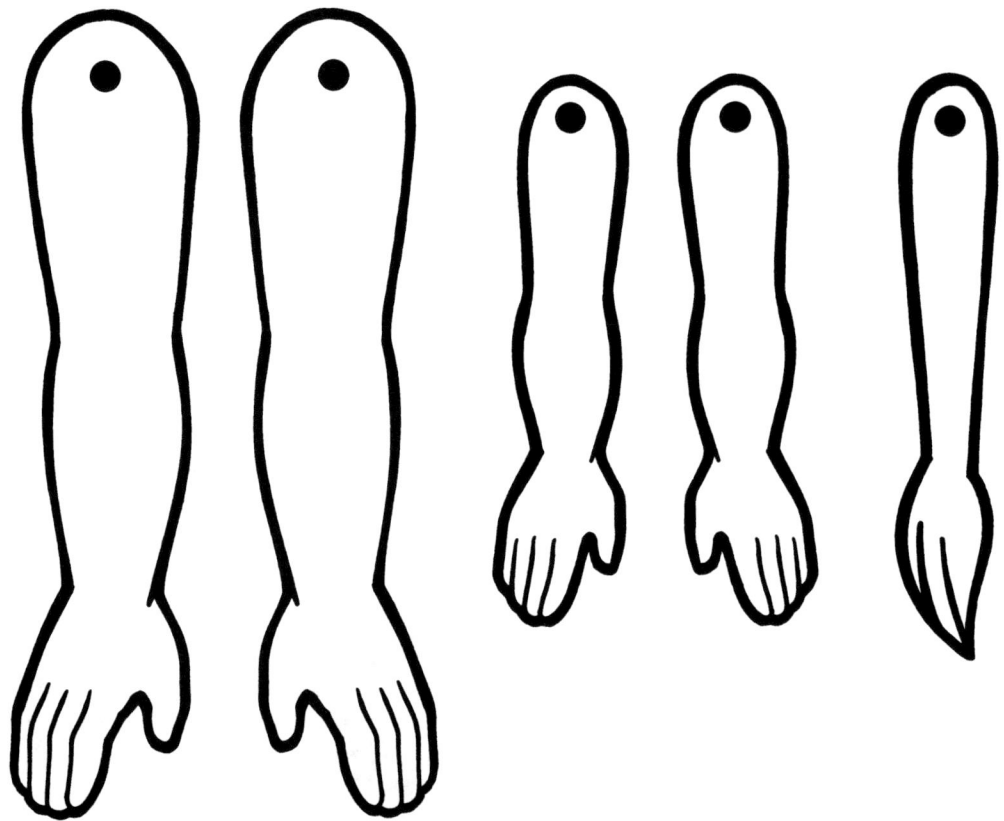

#7061 Bible Stories & Crafts: Animals • 32 • ©Teacher Created Resources

Plagues in Egypt

 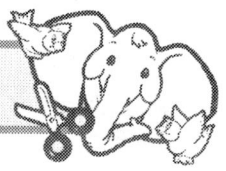

Craft: Moving Picture *(cont.)*

See page 32 for directions.

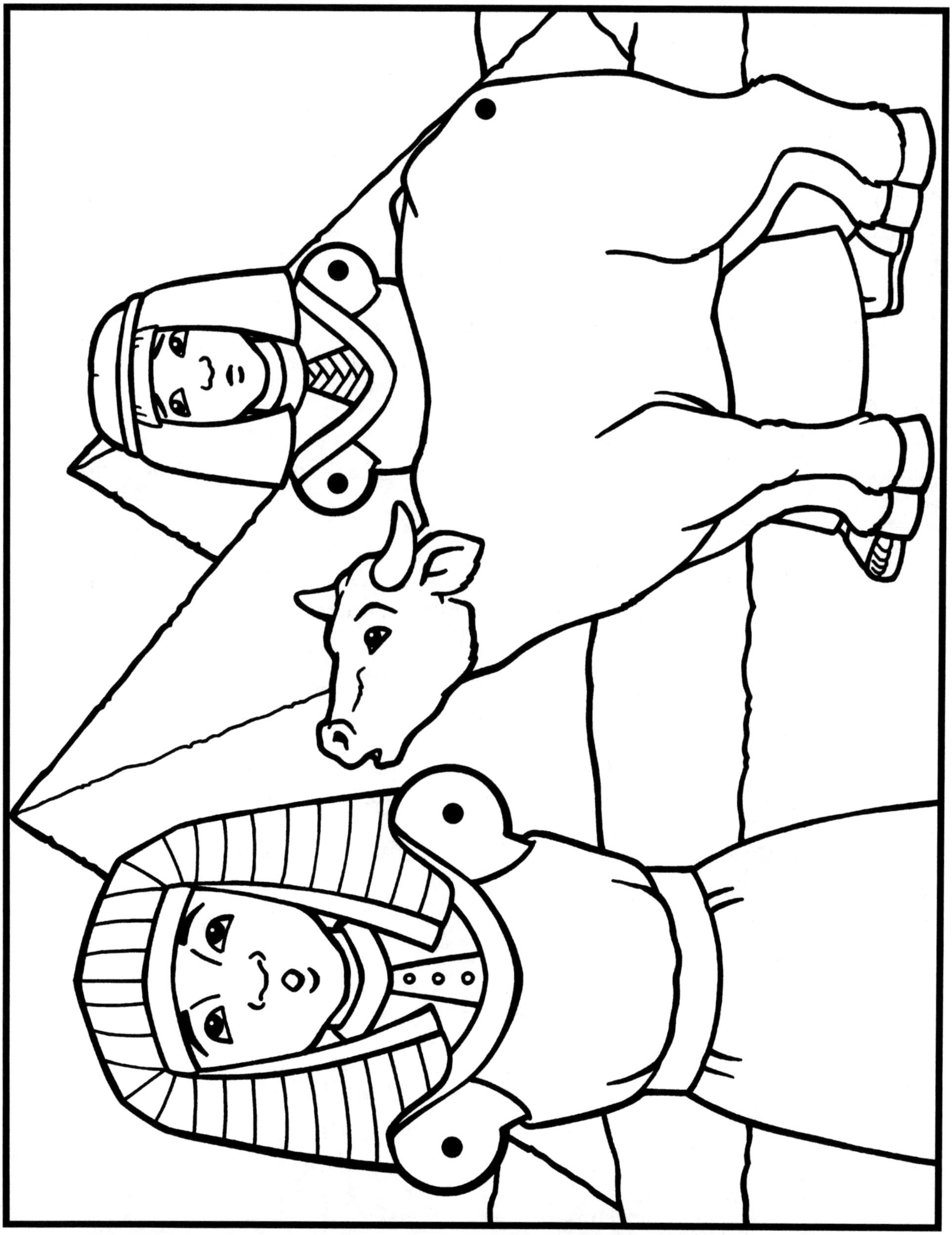

 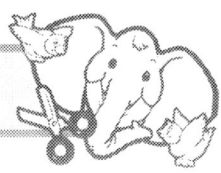

Plagues in Egypt

Craft: Locust Model

Materials

- pattern on page 35
- cardstock or poster board
- crayons, markers, or colored pencils
- paper towel or bathroom tissue tube
- scissors
- hole punch
- tape
- brown or black pipe cleaners

Directions

1. Copy the pattern onto cardstock or poster board.
2. Color the patterns and cut them out.
3. Cut the paper tube to fit the pattern.
4. Wrap the pattern over the paper tube and tape to hold it on the tube.
5. Bend pipe cleaners for back legs.
6. Punch a hole on each side of the tube near the front and stick the pipe cleaner legs in it. Bend each pipe cleaner inside the tube to hold it. (*Optional:* Tape the pipe cleaners inside the tube to secure them.)
7. Cut a pipe cleaner into two shorter pieces for the locust's front legs. Attach them just in front of the back legs in the same way.
8. Cut smaller pieces of pipe cleaner for antennae. Attach the antennae to the front of the head the same way you attach the legs.
9. Let the locust remind students of God's power, which is the same power He uses for them today as He used to send the locusts to plague Egypt.

Finished Product

Plagues in Egypt

Craft: Locust Model *(cont.)*

See page 34 for directions.

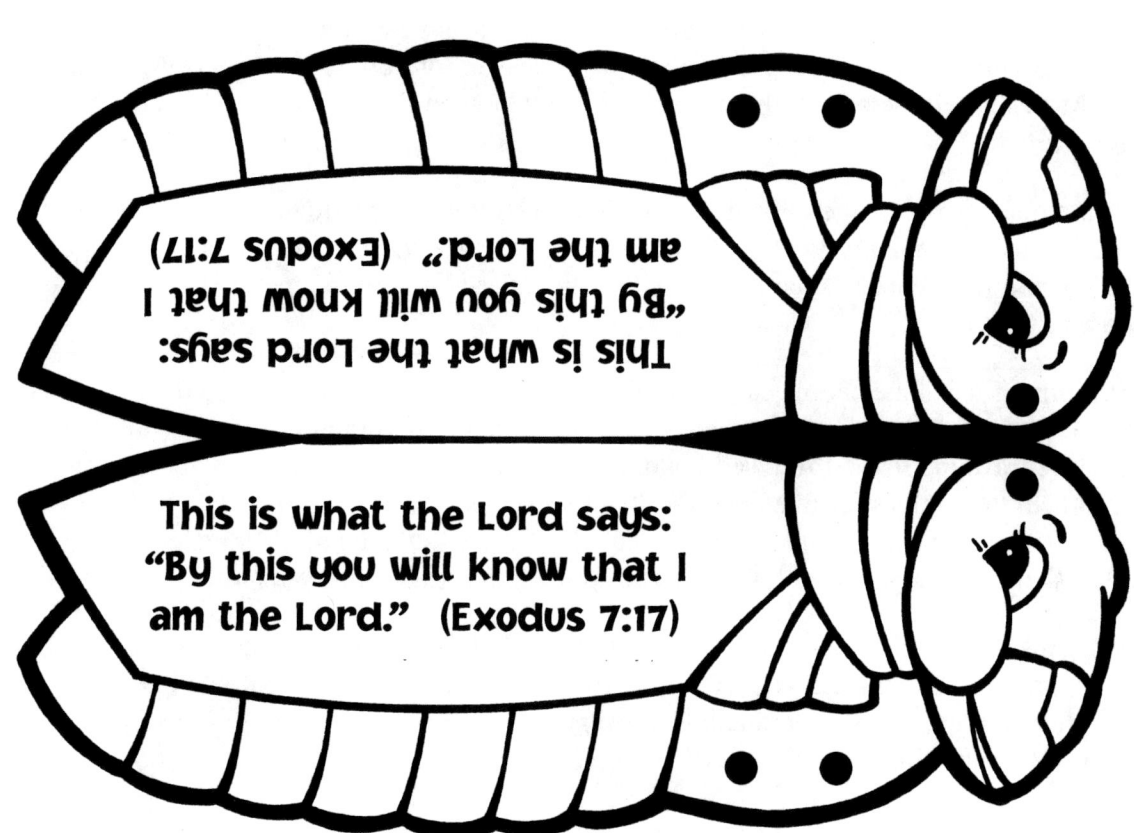

 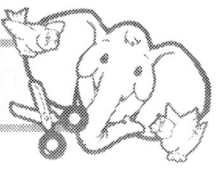

Food for God's People

Bible Story: Exodus 16

As you tell the Bible story, act it out and let children copy your actions.

God had rescued Moses and his people from slavery in Egypt. Now they were traveling across the hot desert to go to the land God had promised them, but the people were not enjoying it! *(Trudge around the room as if your feet are heavy and you're exhausted.)* They were grumbling and complaining to Moses. "If only we had died by the Lord's hand in Egypt!" they said. "There we sat around pots of meat and ate all the food we wanted, but you have brought us out into this desert to starve this entire assembly to death." *(Raise fists and look angry.)* They had quickly forgotten how terrible their lives were in Egypt.

Instead of punishing the people for their complaining, God gave them what they wanted. *(Look toward heaven as if listening.)* "I will rain down bread from heaven for you," He told Moses. Then God instructed Moses to tell the people that in the evening they would have meat to eat. *(Look happy and clap your hands.)*

That evening quail flew into the Israelite camp. The people were able to catch the birds and cook them for a delicious meal. *(Jump around as if chasing and catching quail; then pretend to eat them.)* It was a miracle! There were enough quail to feed everyone, over a million people. *(Raise hands to heaven as if thanking God.)*

The next morning when the people came out of their tents, the ground was covered with thin flakes. This was manna which the Lord gave them to eat every single morning during the whole time the Israelites were traveling to the Promised Land, about 40 years! The people gathered enough each morning to feed themselves for that day. *(Walk around pretending to pick manna off the ground and putting it in a basket; then pretend to eat it.)* The day before the Sabbath they were permitted to gather extra to last them over the Sabbath. God did not provide manna on the Sabbath.

Don't you think the people must have been thankful to God for the miraculous way He provided food for them in the desert? They didn't even bother to thank Him. They just continued to complain about one thing after another. We should thank God every day for all the good things He gives us and never complain just because things aren't exactly the way we want them. *(Fold hands and bow head as if praying.)*

Discussion

- How do you think God felt about His people's grumbling and complaining?
- How was the provision of quail a miracle, and not just a natural occurrence?

Bible Verse

"He rained meat down on them like dust, flying birds like sand on the seashore." (Psalm 78:27)

How does God provide food for you? How often do you thank God for the good things you have to eat?

Food for God's People

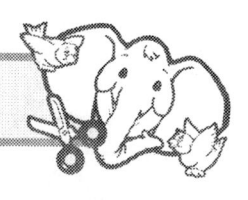

Puppet Skit

Have children make the flying quail puppet on page 38, then use them to act out this skit. Choose a student to be Moses. Divide the other speaking parts among the rest of the students.

Moses:	Listen, everybody! God has told me that He is going to give us meat to eat this evening. I don't know what it will be, but be ready.
Person 1:	I hope it is chicken. I love chicken!
Person 2:	Not me! I would rather have beef. Yummm, I would love a meal of rich, juicy beef.
Person 3:	What makes you think it will be either one, or anything for that matter? Didn't God take us away from Egypt where we had good food to eat and bring us into this desert where we are starving? I do not believe what Moses says. I think God is just going to let us die out here.
Person 4:	Did you get up on the wrong side of the bed this morning or what? We are not starving, and if God says He will give us meat, you can depend on it.
Person 5:	I wonder how it will come. Will somebody bring it in a wagon or on a camel?
Person 6:	I am so hungry I could eat a camel!
Person 7:	I wish God would hurry. I'm really hungry!
Person 8:	Did you hear something?
Person 1:	What? Oh, wait! I hear something, too.
Person 5:	Yes, it is kind of a hand-clapping noise. No, I think it is wings.
Person 6:	It is wings! Look, it is a covey of quails. I do not think I have ever seen so many.
Person 7:	Watch out! They are landing on the ground!
All:	*(Students hold their quail puppets up high and drop them so they twirl to the floor. Then they begin picking them up.)*
Person 4:	Quick! Catch as many as you can.
Person 7:	This is the meat God said He would send us.
Person 3:	No it isn't. This is just a natural thing that happens sometimes. God has nothing to do with it.
Person 2:	I do not care where they came from; I am catching as many as I can.
Person 8:	My family will eat well tonight! I wonder if God really did send these quail.

Craft: Flying Quail Puppet

Materials

- pattern on page 38
- white paper
- crayons, markers, or colored pencils
- scissors
- tape

Food for God's People

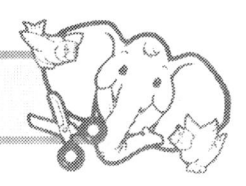

Craft: Flying Quail Puppet *(cont.)*

Directions

1. Copy the quail pattern onto white paper.
2. Then color the quail pattern and cut it out. Also, be sure to cut down the middle.
3. Fold back the two side tabs and tape them in back of the head.
4. Fold one wing back and the other forward over the head at the dashed lines.
5. Hold the quail up high by the head and drop it. It will twirl to the floor.
6. Use the quail puppet to act out the puppet story on page 37.

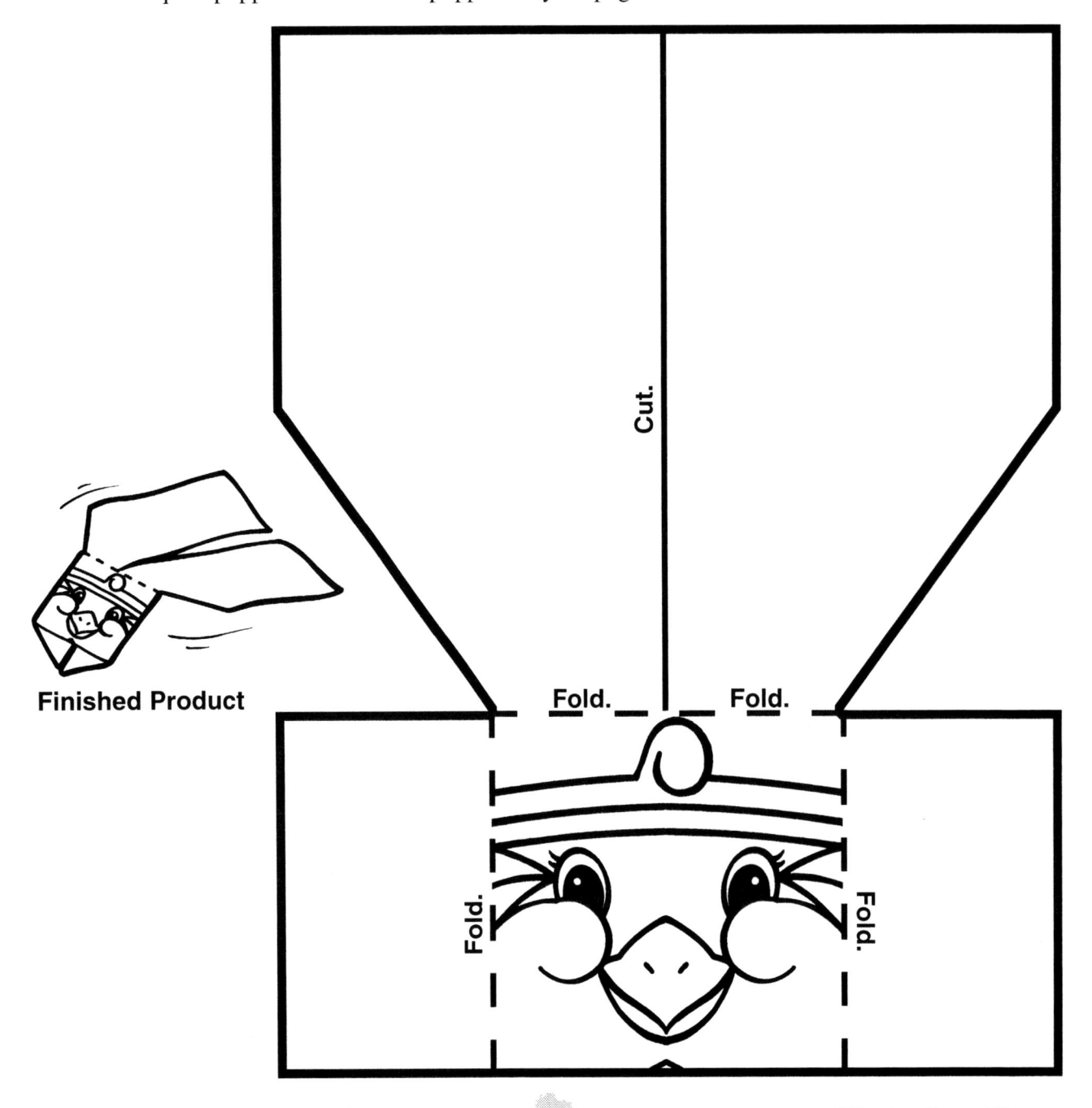

Finished Product

#7061 Bible Stories & Crafts: Animals ©Teacher Created Resources

Food for God's People

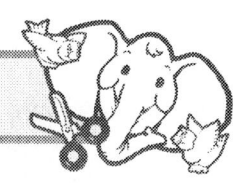

Craft: Quail Fan

Materials

- pattern and word strip below
- cardstock or poster board
- crayons, markers, or colored pencils
- large wooden craft sticks or tongue depressors
- clear adhesive plastic
- scissors
- glue

Directions

1. Copy the pattern onto white cardstock paper or poster board.
2. Color the pattern.
3. Cover the pattern with clear adhesive plastic.
4. Cut out the pattern.
5. Glue it onto a large craft stick or tongue depressor (for a handle).
6. Cut out the word strip and glue it to the quail's wings.

Finished Product

God gives His children whatever they need.

©Teacher Created Resources   #7061 Bible Stories & Crafts: Animals

Food for God's People

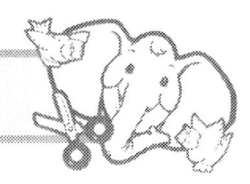

Craft: Quail Verse Reminder

Materials

- patterns below
- cardstock or poster board
- crayons, markers, or colored pencils
- scissors
- tape or brad fastener
- feathers *(optional)*

Finished Product

Directions

1. Copy the patterns onto cardstock or poster board.
2. Color the patterns.
3. Cut out the patterns and use a brad fastener to attach the wing at the top (or tape it).
4. Flip the wing open to reveal the verse. (*Optional:* Glue feathers to the wing.)

"My God will meet all your needs according to his glorious riches in Christ Jesus." (Philippians 4:19)

#7061 Bible Stories & Crafts: Animals

©Teacher Created Resources

Ark of the Covenant Comes Home

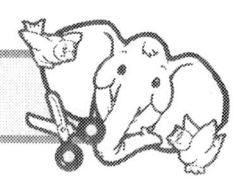

Bible Story: 1 Samuel 4-6

Explain to your students that you want them to help you tell the Bible story by repeating a sentence every time you hold up your right hand. Print the words on the board to help them remember: "And the cows kept pulling the cart."

One day the Israelites were fighting a fierce battle with their enemies, the Philistines. Every Israelite soldier fought with all his might, but the Philistines won the battle. They could not understand why the Lord had allowed them to be defeated. They decided to send for the Ark of the Covenant to be brought to them before their next battle. Surely if the ark were there, the Lord would be with them! The Ark of the Covenant was a special box that God had ordered to be kept in the holiest part of the tabernacle. Inside the box were some of the manna God had given His people in the wilderness, Aaron's rod, and the tablets on which God Himself had written the Ten Commandments.

How excited the soldiers were when the ark arrived. They shouted excitedly. When the Philistine soldiers found out what the Israelites had done, they became frightened. "A god has come into their camp," they said. The Philistines did not believe in the Israelites' God, but they felt there must be some kind of magic attached to the Ark of the Covenant. The Philistines fought even more fiercely in the next battle and once again beat the Israelites. To make matters worse, they stole the ark!

All Israelites everywhere were shocked and sad to hear that the idol-worshiping Philistines had stolen their ark and put it on display in one of their idol's temples. The Philistines were starting to believe that they should not have taken the ark because strange things had begun to happen as soon as they brought it home. Their idol, which sat next to the ark, kept falling on its face and finally was broken. Nobody could explain why! Then the people who lived in the area where the ark was displayed suddenly became very sick and many died. They decided to move the ark to another town, but when they did, the people of that town also became sick and died. When it was decided to move the ark to a third town, the people who lived there cried out, "Send the ark of the god of Israel away; let it go back to its own place, or it will kill us and our people!"

Finally, the Philistines decided to send the Ark of the Covenant back to the Israelites. But how? No one wanted to take it into enemy territory. Most Philistines were even afraid to be near the ark! They planned carefully how to get it back in the safest way. Two cows were chosen to pull the ark on a cart. They would be on their own with no one to drive them. Would they go where they were supposed to go? The ark was set securely on the cart, the two cows were hitched to the cart, and the cows began walking toward Israel. Some Philistines followed the cows to the border to make sure nothing went wrong to keep it in their own land. But the cows did not stop. *(Raise right hand so students say, "And the cows kept pulling the cart.")* Both cows had calves that had been left behind. They were not happy to be separated from their babies, but they did not stop. *(Raise right hand.)* The cows had never been to Israel, so they did not really know where they were going. *(Raise right hand.)* Cows are not used to pulling carts, especially with no one to direct them. *(Raise right hand.)* The cows kept heading toward Israel and did not turn to the right or left. *(Raise right hand.)* The sun was hot and the cows must have been thirsty. *(Raise right hand.)*

Some Israelites were working in their fields harvesting wheat when they saw a strange sight—two cows pulling a cart with no driver! *(Raise right hand.)* Suddenly, the cows stopped. The people ran over and shouted with joy when they saw that their Ark of the Covenant was on the cart! They took it off the cart and offered burnt sacrifices to the Lord. Unfortunately for the cows, they were the sacrifices!

Ark of the Covenant Comes Home

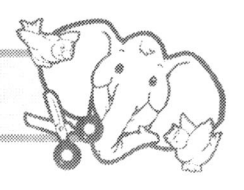

Discussion

- Why is it sometimes hard to pray?
- Which is better—to pray at a certain time each day or to pray off and on throughout the day? Why?
- How can praying for other people actually help us get along with people better?
- What should we do when we don't feel like praying?

Bible Verse

"Do not be anxious about anything, but in everything, by prayer and petition, with thanksgiving, present your requests to God." (Philippians 4:6)

How often do you pray? Why not start the day with God by praying as soon as you wake up each morning and end the day with God by praying before you go to sleep each night? Talk to Him about anything and everything in your life. He wants to hear from you.

Puppet Skit

Follow the directions on page 43 to make cow paper bag puppets. Divide children into three cow groups with only two cows in group 3. Have them use their paper bag puppets as they read the following skit.

Group 1: Mooo! Mooo! Why have these men gathered us cows together? What's going on? What do they want us to do?

Group 2: Maww! Maww! I want my mother! Why won't they let us calves be with our moms?

Group 1: Mooove over! The men are choosing those two cows to do something. Where are they going?

Group 3: Mooo! Mooo! I do not want to pull this cart. I want to stay here with my baby! Mooo!

Group 2: Maww! Maww! I want my mom!

Group 1: There they go. Goodbye! I wonder where they are going?

Group 3: Mooo! Why did they have to choose me for this job? Mooo! I do not want to . . . wait a minute! I think my Creator wants me to do this. He is leading me somewhere. I guess I'd better follow Him.

Group 1: Look at them go! They act like they know right where they are going.

Group 3: I do not know where I am going or why, but the One who made me is in charge of me. I must follow Him and do what he wants. I won't turn around or go back. I'll keep going until He wants me to stop.

#7061 Bible Stories & Crafts: Animals ©Teacher Created Resources

Ark of the Covenant Comes Home

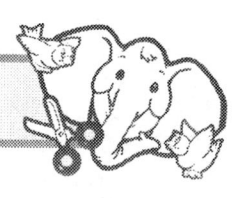

Craft: Paper Bag Cow Puppet

Materials

- patterns below
- paper lunch bag
- crayons or colored markers
- scissors
- glue

Directions

1. Color the patterns and cut them out.
2. Glue the cow's head to the flat bottom of the bag.
3. Glue the tongue beneath the bottom flap.
4. Put your hand inside the bag and make the cow talk.

Finished Product

©Teacher Created Resources

#7061 Bible Stories & Crafts: Animals

Ark of the Covenant Comes Home

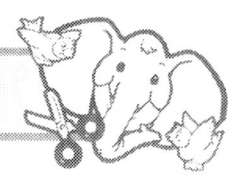

Craft: Moving Picture

Materials

- patterns on pages 44 and 45
- cardstock or poster board
- crayons, markers, or colored pencils
- craft stick
- scissors
- glue

Directions

1. Copy the patterns onto cardstock or poster board.
2. Color the patterns and cut them out.
3. Cut a slit across the picture where indicated.
4. Glue the cows and wagon to the end of the craft stick.
5. Push the craft stick up through the slit and move the cows and wagon across the picture from the back.

Finished Product

#7061 Bible Stories & Crafts: Animals ©Teacher Created Resources

Ark of the Covenant Comes Home

Craft: Moving Picture *(cont.)*

Ark of the Covenant Comes Home

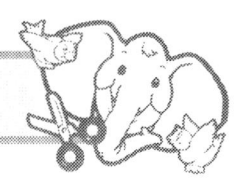

Craft: Movable Cow

Materials

- patterns below
- cardstock or poster board
- crayons, markers, or colored pencils
- brad fasteners
- scissors
- hole punch

Finished Product

Directions

1. Copy the patterns onto cardstock or poster board.
2. Color the patterns and cut them out.
3. Punch holes where indicated with a hole punch.
4. Use the brad fasteners to attach the body parts to the cow.

Who controls everything? (God)

"Ask the animals, and they will teach you." (Job 12:7a)

#7061 Bible Stories & Crafts: Animals ©Teacher Created Resources

Solomon's Riches

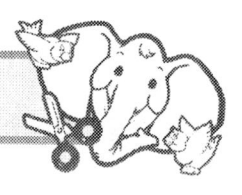

Bible Story: 1 Kings 10

As you tell about Solomon's riches, list his possessions on the board for everyone to see.

Solomon, David's son, was the wisest king who ever lived. He was also the richest. The Queen of Sheba, another very rich ruler, traveled to Jerusalem to check out King Solomon's wisdom by asking him some hard questions. She was amazed! "She said to the king, 'The report I heard in my own country about your achievements and your wisdom is true. But I did not believe these things until I came and saw with my own eyes. Indeed, not even half was told to me; in wisdom and wealth you have far exceeded the report I heard. Praise be to the Lord your God, who has delighted in you and placed you on the throne of Israel.'" (I Kings 10:6–7, 9a)

Before she left, the Queen of Sheba added to Solomon's riches by giving him gifts of gold and spices and jewels. Solomon already had plenty of these things, but he kept getting more! Every year he received more than 4½ tons of gold (truckloads full). He used some of the gold to make 200 large shields and 300 small shields which he kept in his palace. He had a special gold and ivory throne made for himself. It had six steps leading up to it with two figures of lions on each step. Nobody had ever seen anything like it!

He drank from golden goblets and ate from plates of gold. He had a fleet of trading ships that sailed everywhere, bringing him more gold, silver, and ivory. They also brought interesting and unusual animals such as apes and baboons.

Everyone wanted to be able to talk to Solomon and see his wisdom for themselves. And everyone who came to visit him brought gifts—gold, silver, robes, weapons, spices, horses, and mules. King Solomon loved horses. He imported the most beautiful, strong horses from Egypt. He soon had 12,000 horses and 1,400 chariots. But the horses became a problem. One of God's rules for His people said: "The king, moreover, must not acquire great numbers of horses for himself." (See Deuteronomy 17:16a.) God wanted His people to trust Him to protect them. He knew that strong military forces, such as many horses and chariots, would make the people turn away from Him and begin trusting in their own ability to fight.

King Solomon ignored this rule and many others. Sure enough, the more horses and gold and riches of all kinds he got, the more he turned away from God. Before long, he was worshipping idols with his many wives and trying to say he trusted God, too. Though God blessed him with great wisdom and riches, Solomon failed God. After his death the kingdom was split and taken away from Solomon's family.

Discussion

- Though Solomon was the wisest king who ever lived, he did not seem to be very wise about how to use his riches. What could he have done with his riches that would have pleased God more?

- Which is better—to have all the money you could ever want, or to do God's will?

Solomon's Riches

Bible Verse

"Some trust in chariots and some in horses, but we trust in the name of the Lord our God." (Psalm 20:7)

What are some other things people sometimes trust in? Why is trusting in God better?

Puppet Skit

Follow the directions on page 49 to make horse stick puppets. Let students use them to act out the following skit. Choose a child to read the part of King Solomon and one to be the narrator. The other children can be horses, moving their stick puppets to make them run and making horse noises.

Solomon:	Ah, just look at them! What a beautiful, strong group of horses! I think they are the best yet.
Horses:	(*Running and making horse noises.*)
Solomon:	Let me see now, how many does this make in my stables? I must have about 12,000 horses now. And I would love to have more. You can never have too many horses.
Horses:	(*Running and making horse noises.*)
Solomon:	With all these horses and the chariots I own, I feel very safe. I do not think there is an army anywhere that could defeat Israel with all this power behind us.
Narrator:	God had a rule for Israel's kings. He said they were not to have great numbers of horses, for if they did, they would begin to trust in their military power instead of in Him. King Solomon had ignored God's rule.
Solomon:	What a powerful nation we are! We do not need to worry about other armies. Run, my beautiful horses! You will keep us safe, won't you?
Horses:	(*Running and making horse noises.*)
Narrator:	Solomon had forgotten that it was God who had made him wise and rich and powerful, and God was the one who would keep Israel safe.

Solomon's Riches

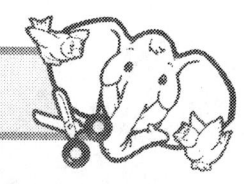

Craft: Horse Stick Puppets

Materials

- patterns below
- crayons or colored markers
- scissors
- cardstock
- craft sticks
- glue or tape

Directions

1. Copy the horse patterns onto cardstock.
2. Color the horses and cut them out.
3. Glue or tape each horse to the end of a craft stick for a handle.

Finished Product

Solomon's Riches

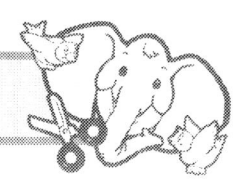

Craft: 3-D Horse Picture

Materials

- patterns below and on page 51
- cardstock or poster board
- crayons, markers, or colored pencils
- scissors
- glue

Directions

1. Copy the patterns onto cardstock or poster board.
2. Color the patterns and the picture and cut them out.
3. Cut out three strips and fold them accordion style and then glue behind the horses.
4. Glue the horses on the picture.

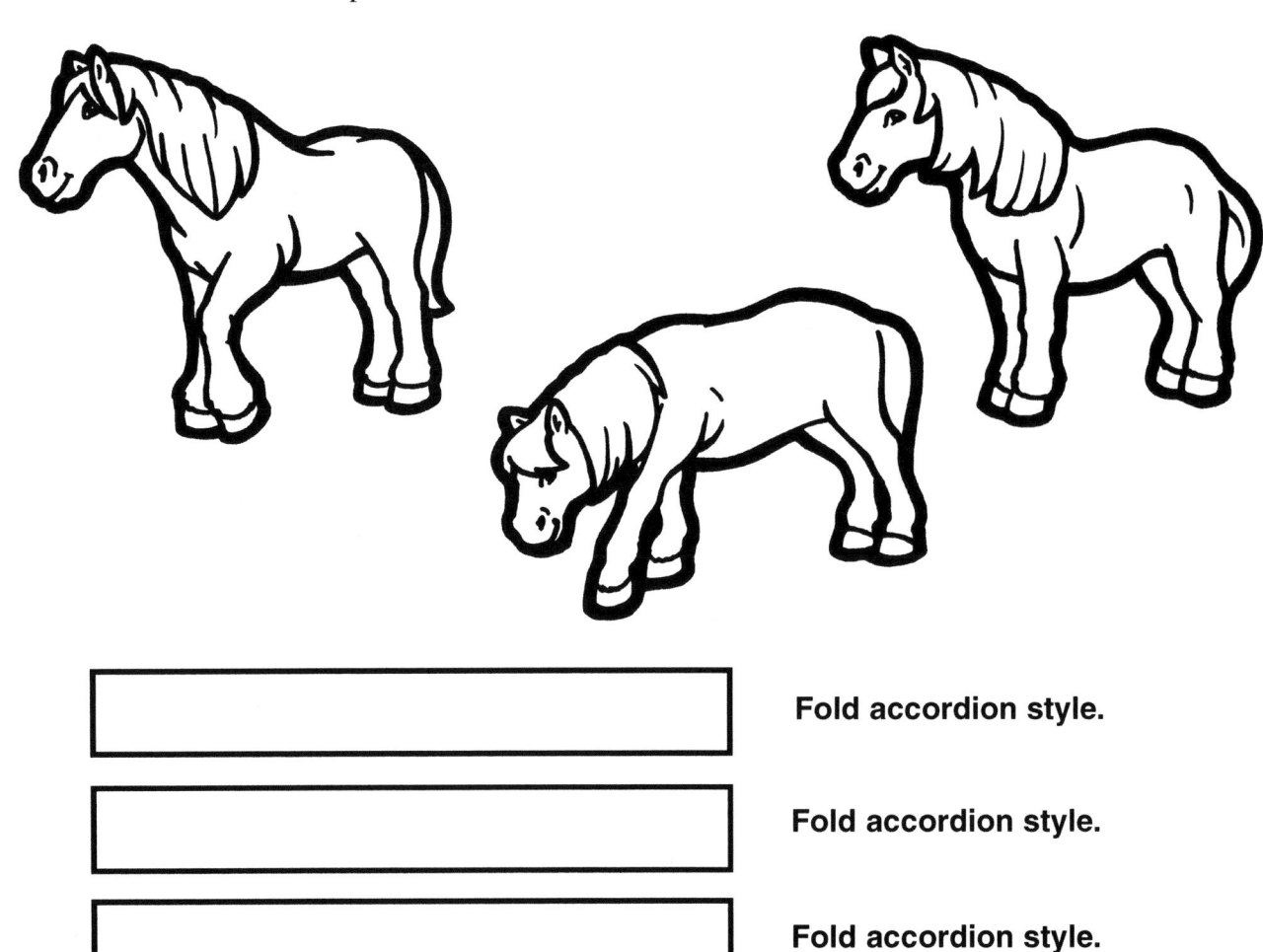

Finished Product

Fold accordion style.

Fold accordion style.

Fold accordion style.

Solomon's Riches

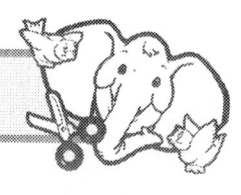

Craft: 3-D Horse Picture *(cont.)*

"His pleasure is not in the strength of the horse, nor his delight in the legs of a man; the Lord delights in those who fear him." (Psalm 147:10–11a)

Solomon's Riches

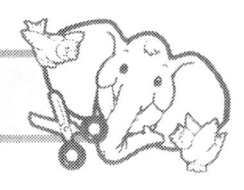

Craft: Horseshoes

Materials
- patterns and verse strip below
- cardstock or poster board
- crayons, markers, or colored pencils
- yarn
- scissors
- glue
- hole punch

Directions
1. Copy the patterns onto cardstock or poster board.
2. Color the patterns. Then cut out the horseshoes and verse strip.
3. Overlap the two horseshoes and glue as shown. Then glue the verse strip on top of the horseshoes.
4. Punch holes on each side of the horseshoes and tie yarn to the horseshoes to hang.

Finished Product

"Some trust in chariots and some in horses, but we trust in the name of the Lord our God."
(Psalm 20:7)

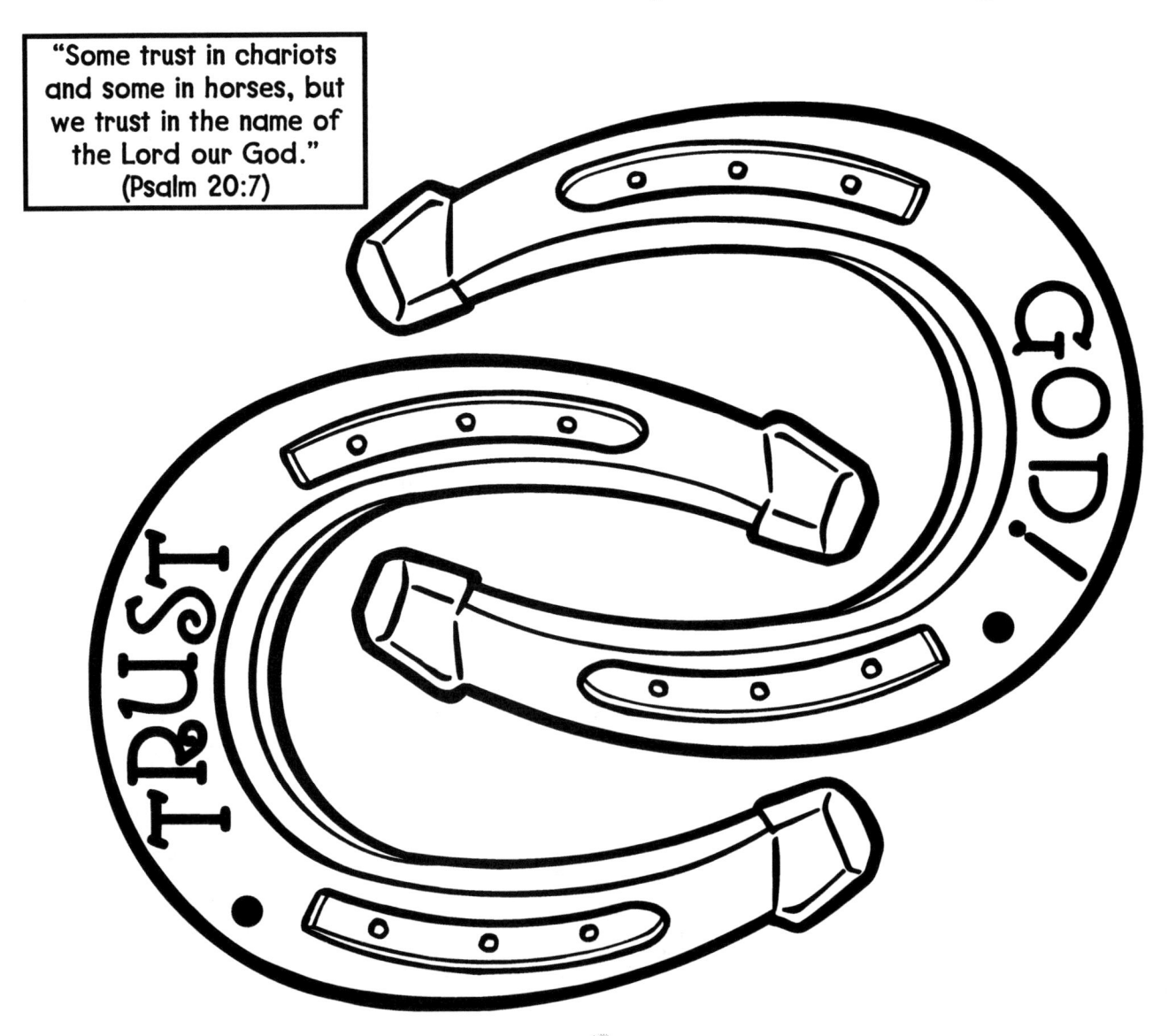

TRUST GOD!

#7061 Bible Stories & Crafts: Animals · ©Teacher Created Resources

Solomon Talks About Hard Work

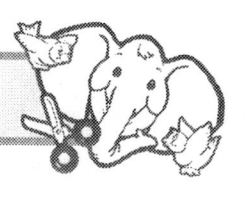

Bible Story: Proverbs 6:6-11; 30:24-25

If possible, bring some ants in a jar for children to observe. As you talk about ants, ask questions for the children to answer.

Raise your hand if you like ants. Why do you like them? (*Let students share their ideas.*) Why don't most people like ants? (*Let students share their ideas. Point out the trouble ants cause, invading kitchens, crawling on food, etc.*) Most of us do not think twice about stepping on ants when they are crawling on the sidewalk. Actually, we hardly notice them most of the time because they are so much smaller than we are. But the wisest king the world ever knew noticed ants. What was his name? (*Solomon*)

King Solomon was wise and powerful and very, very rich. He lived in a beautiful, huge palace. He had people from other countries visiting him all the time, bringing him gifts. He had hundreds of wives. But even with all that was going on in his life, Solomon took time to notice a tiny insect. He found ants very interesting and wrote about them in two different places in his book of Proverbs. A proverb is a wise saying, such as "An apple a day keeps the doctor away." Solomon's proverbs were about living the way God wants us to.

What do ants have to do with living the way God wants us to? What do you think we can learn by watching ants? (*Let students share their ideas.*) One of Solomon's proverbs says, "Go to the ant, you sluggard; consider its ways and be wise." What do you think a sluggard is? (*Let students share their ideas.*) A sluggard is a person who is lazy, not just now and then, but all the time. Solomon said that lazy people could learn something important from ants. He pointed out that ants do not have anybody who makes them work. They do not have teachers or bosses or kings to make them do anything. But they work hard, all on their own. In the summer and fall, ants are always busy gathering food and storing it away for the winter. Have you ever seen an ant carrying a large crumb or piece of food? An ant can carry 20 times its own weight. Of course, most ants are tiny, so they cannot carry very big things. If you were strong enough to carry something 20 times what you weigh, how heavy a load could you lift? (*Let students multiply 20 times their body weight to figure out what they could carry.*) Could you lift a 50-pound bag of dog or cat food? Could you pick up your mom or dad? How many people in this class could you carry at once?

Ants are strong for their size. They do not use their strength to play games or go to the gym to work out. What do they use their strength for? (*Let students share their ideas.*) They use their strength to work hard to gather food and protect the other ants in their colony.

Solomon also said that ants are very wise, and he was a man who knew about wisdom! Though they have tiny brains compared to ours and most of them only live for about two months, somehow they figure out ways to find food, build nests, and protect one another. And ants are tidy. Some ants have the job of taking out the trash! They are responsible for cleaning the nest and throwing away the trash. Ants know the value of cooperation. They always work together because they can accomplish more that way. Do you know how to cooperate with others to get things done? (*Let students share.*)

From now on when you see an ant, remember Solomon's words. Do not be lazy. Work hard and do your best for yourself and your family and friends. If a tiny ant can do it, you certainly can. Can't you?

Solomon Talks About Hard Work

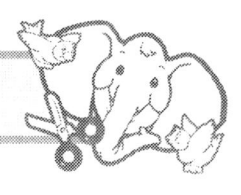

Discussion

- Who gives ants their strength and wisdom?
- Who gives you strength and wisdom?
- What do you think God expects you to do with what He gives you?
- How can you show your thanks to Him for the abilities He has given you?

Bible Verse

"Go to the ant, you sluggard; consider its ways and be wise!" (Proverbs 6:6)

The Bible teaches us that God does not approve of laziness. He wants us to be busy working for Him, even when no one is telling us what to do.

Puppet Skit

Follow the directions on page 55 to make magnet puppets. Let children use them to act out the skit. Lay a long sheet of paper on a table. Have children draw a scene which includes a piece of cake on the ground near a creek. Have them draw small hills, valleys, and trees in a grassy field. Have two people hold up the scene by each end. Children can attach their magnet puppets to the scene and stand behind it to manipulate them from the back as you read the skit. Let them speak the parts of the ants.

Narrator:	One day the ants in a green field got excited. One of the ant workers had discovered leftover food from a picnic over by the creek.
Ants:	Let's go get it!
Narrator:	The ants began pouring out of their nest, following the ant who knew where the food was. All the ants moved in a neat line and no one tried to run ahead. They crawled over hills and around trees, under plants and through grass. The sun was hot and the creek seemed far away, but the ants kept going. They were almost there; they could smell it! Soon they found the food. Some human had left behind a big piece of cake. Wow!
Ants:	Yum, yum, yum!
Narrator:	Now what would be the best way to get the cake back to their nest? One ant tried to pick up the cake, but it was too big for him to lift. A few more went to help him, but it was still too heavy. Then one of the ants went over to the cake and picked off a crumb of it, just the right size for him to carry. He turned around and headed back across the field to the nest with his load. Other ants began doing the same and soon there was a long line of ants carrying cake crumbs headed across the field. Bit by bit, that piece of cake was taken to the ants' nest. No one stopped to rest or play. Each ant did its best. When an ant reached the nest and dropped off his cake crumb, he turned around and headed back across the field to get another crumb. It took a long time, but the cake was finally all gone!

Solomon Talks About Hard Work

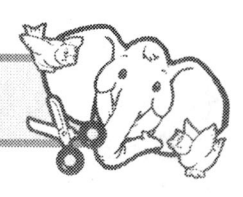

Craft: Ant Magnet Puppets

Materials

- patterns below
- cardstock
- scissors
- glue
- small magnets

Directions

1. Copy the ant patterns onto cardstock.
2. Cut out the ants.
3. Glue a small magnet to the back of each ant. Each child will need two ants, each going in a different direction.
4. Place each ant magnet on the paper scene described on page 54. Hold it on with one hand while you place another magnet in the same place on the back of the paper scene. To make the ant move, gently move the magnet on the back of the scene. Use all the ants going in the same direction for the trip to the cake, then switch to ants going the other direction for the return trip to the nest.

Finished Product

©Teacher Created Resources   #7061 Bible Stories & Crafts: Animals

Solomon Talks About Hard Work

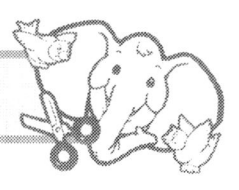

Craft: Ants Plaque

Materials

- patterns below
- cardstock or poster board
- crayons or markers
- colored yarn or ribbon
- scissors with decorative edges
- construction paper
- glue
- hole punch

Finished Product

Directions

1. Copy the patterns onto cardstock or poster board.
2. Color the patterns and cut them out. (Use scissors with decorative edges to cut out the poem.)
3. Glue the poem to the background piece.
4. Use a hole punch to punch holes where indicated.
5. Weave ribbon or yarn through the holes, then tie the ends in a bow.
6. Glue the completed piece to a contrasting color of construction paper.
7. Glue ants around the border of the plaque.

Ants work hard at everything they do.

Be like the ants and do your very best too!

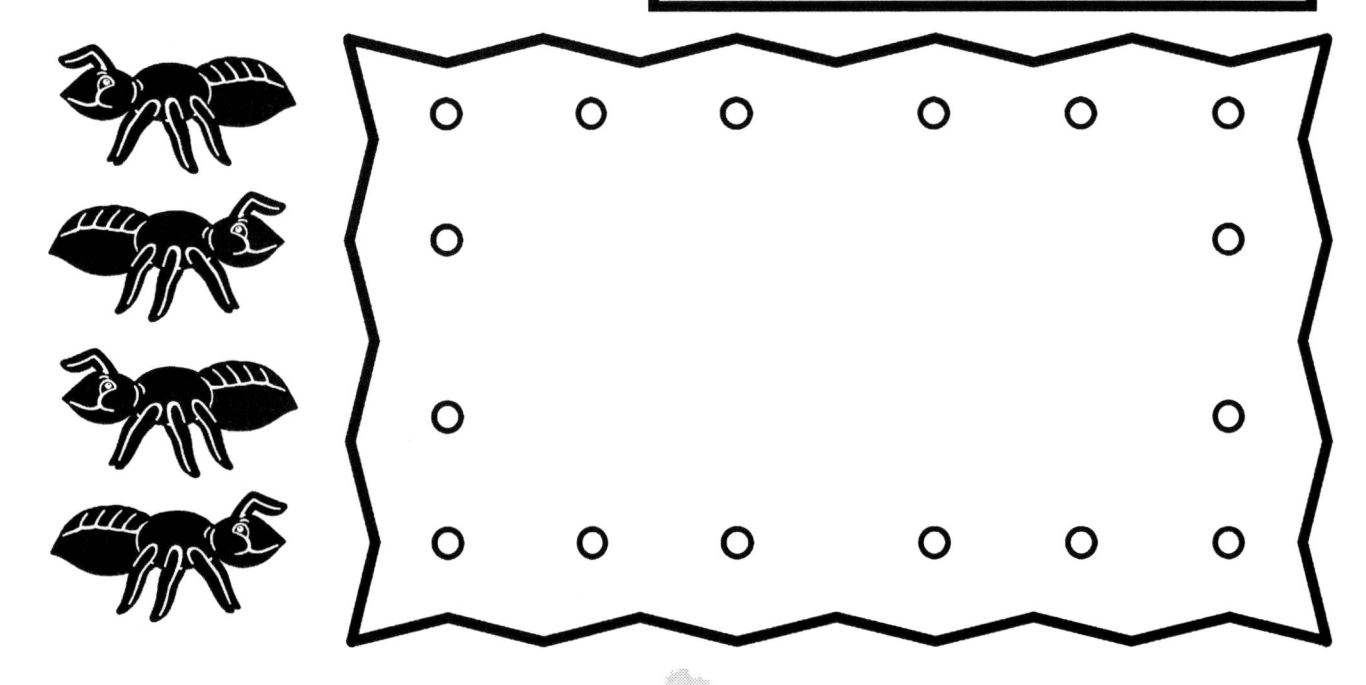

#7061 Bible Stories & Crafts: Animals — ©Teacher Created Resources

Solomon Talks About Hard Work

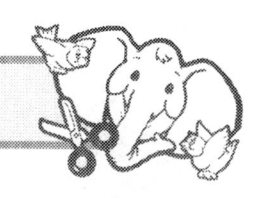

Craft: Picnic Picture

Materials

- patterns below
- picnic scene on page 58
- cardstock or poster board
- crayons, markers, or colored pencils
- yellow paper
- scissors
- cotton balls
- glue

Finished Product

Directions

1. Copy the picnic scene on page 58 and all patterns below (except the sun) onto cardstock or poster board and cut them out.
2. Copy the sun onto yellow paper and cut it out.
3. Color the picnic scene.
4. Glue the ants and sun on the picnic scene.
5. Cut out the Bible verse cloud and glue it to the picnic scene.
6. Glue cotton balls around the cloud verse.
7. Add the other cloud and cotton balls as space allows.

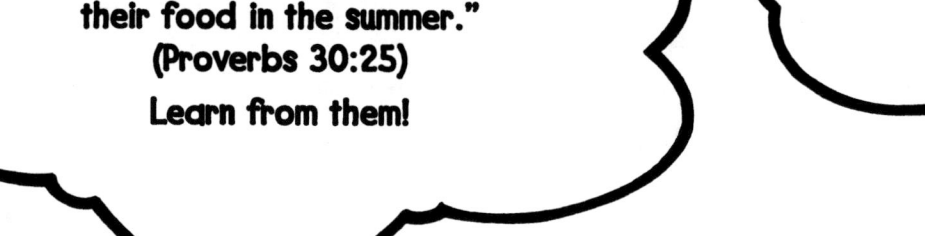

"Ants are creatures of little strength, yet they store up their food in the summer." (Proverbs 30:25)
Learn from them!

©Teacher Created Resources　　57　　#7061 Bible Stories & Crafts: Animals

Solomon Talks About Hard Work

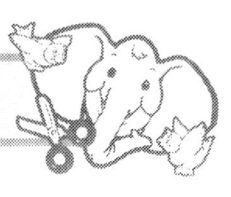

Craft: Picnic Picture *(cont.)*

#7061 Bible Stories & Crafts: Animals 58 ©Teacher Created Resources

Elijah and the Ravens

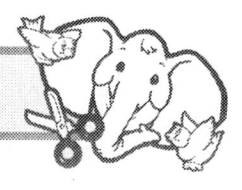

Bible Story: 1 Kings 17:1-6

Have children copy your actions as you tell the story in this action rhyme.

Elijah went to see Ahab the king.

(Walk in place, then bow slightly from the waist.)

He said, "A message from God is what I bring.

(Point up toward heaven.)

A drought is coming; it's almost here.

(Gesture with arm.)

It will not rain for the next few years."

(Wiggle fingers like raindrops falling down.)

Then God told Elijah, "Do what I say.

(Look up and hold hand next to ear as if listening.)

Go to Kerith Brook; do it right away.

(Point far away and shake head yes.)

You can drink from the brook, and bread and meat

(Pretend to drink from cupped hands and rub stomach.)

Will be brought by ravens; you'll have plenty to eat."

(Flap arms as if flying.)

Elijah obeyed for He trusted God's word.

(Bow head as if praying.)

Who but God would think to feed a man from a bird?

(Point to heaven, then yourself, then raise hands and shrug shoulders.)

Elijah and the Ravens

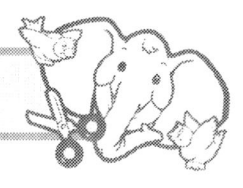

Discussion

Ravens are birds similar to crows. They will eat almost anything. So why do you think they did not eat the food, but brought it to Elijah instead? Some interesting Bible stories are about unusual ways God used animals. Can you think of some others? *(Daniel in the lions' den, Jonah and the great fish, Balaam's donkey)* What do these kinds of stories teach us about God?

Bible Verse

"And my God will meet all your needs according to his glorious riches in Christ Jesus." (Philippians 4:19)

Has God ever provided for you in an unusual way? Has he used an animal to teach you something?

Puppet Skit

Follow the directions on page 61 to make raven puppets. Let children use them to act out the skit. You can read the part of Elijah and the children can be the ravens bringing food to you.

Elijah:	Lord, here I am at the brook where you told me to go. I am tired and hungry, but I believe you will provide food for me here because You said You would. Now I am going to sleep. Goodnight, Lord. *(Sit down in a chair, lean back, and pretend to sleep. After a few moments, open your eyes and stretch as if waking up.)* What a beautiful morning. I need a drink. *(Lean down and pretend to get water from the brook in your cupped hands, then bring it to your mouth and pretend to drink.)* I wonder what time my breakfast will arrive.
Ravens:	Caw, caw, caw! Here comes your breakfast, Elijah! *(Fly puppets down to Elijah.)*
Elijah:	Mmmmm, that's good bread. Boy, I was hungry! Thank you, ravens. I will see you again this evening.
Ravens:	Caw, caw, caw! We will be back, Elijah! Caw, caw! *(Fly puppets away from Elijah.)*
Elijah:	Was that my stomach growling? It must be time for dinner. Yes, I hear the ravens coming!
Ravens:	Caw, caw, caw! It is dinnertime, Elijah. Here we come with meat for you to eat. Caw, caw! *(Fly puppets down to Elijah.)*
Elijah:	Dear God, thank You for sending this food to me. I know if it weren't for You, these hungry ravens would eat it themselves. Thank You for using them to feed me instead. And thank you, ravens!
Ravens:	Caw, caw, caw! You are welcome. We will eat your leftovers if you can not eat it all. Caw, caw!

Elijah and the Ravens

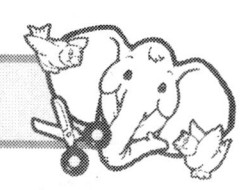

Craft: Raven Puppet

Materials

- pattern below
- white paper
- transparent tape
- scissors

Directions

1. Copy the raven pattern on white paper and cut it out.
2. Fold the pattern in half.
3. Fold down the wings so they flap.
4. Tape the body of the raven together with a piece of tape on top of the head and another piece of tape at the top between the wing and the tail.
5. Then release the bird in the air and watch it fly.

Finished Product

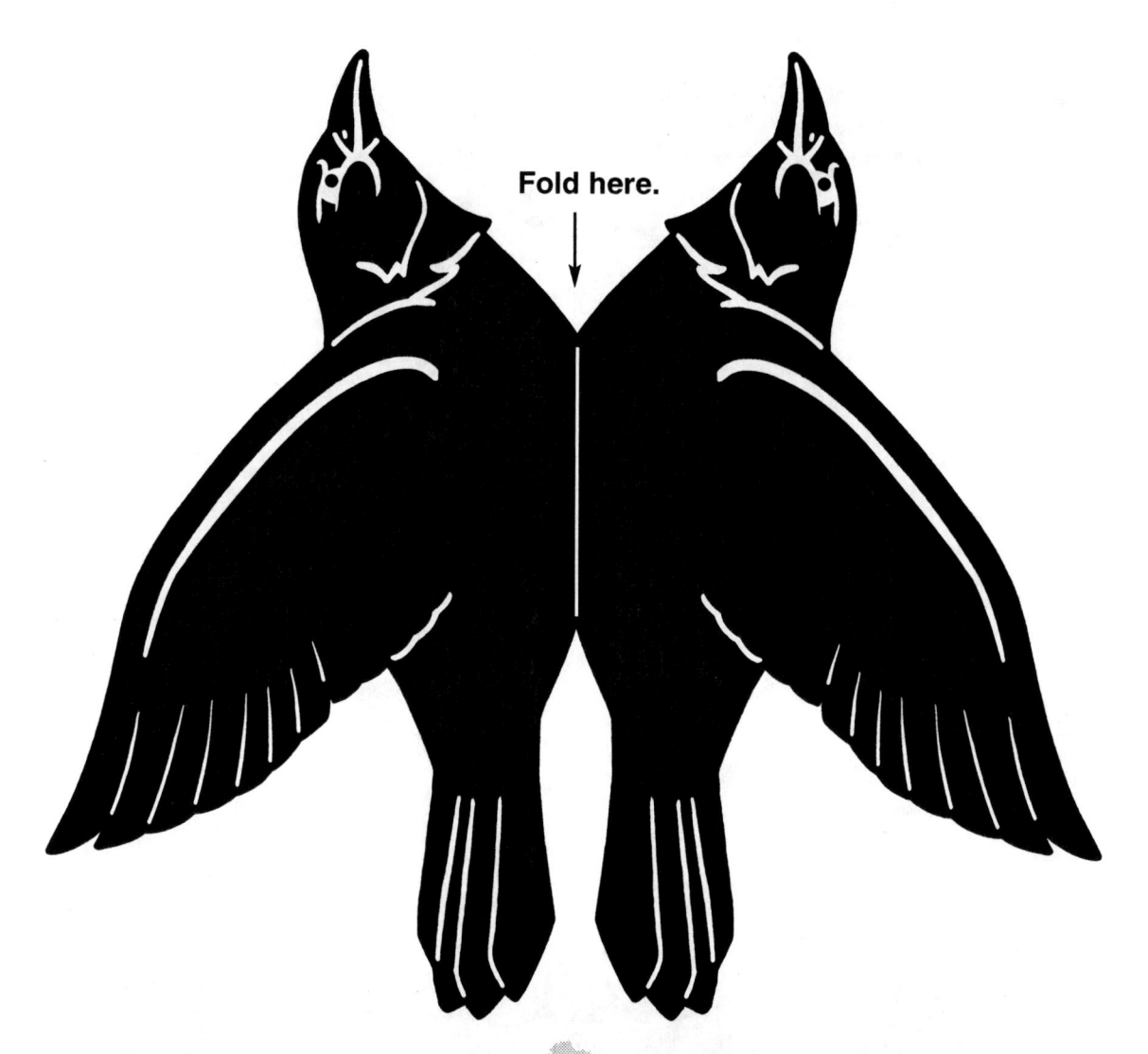

Fold here.

©Teacher Created Resources   61   #7061 Bible Stories & Crafts: Animals

Elijah and the Ravens

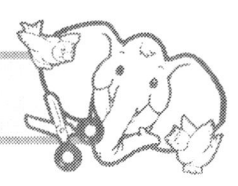

Craft: Bible Verse Raven

Materials

- pattern and verse cards on pages 62 and 63
- cardstock or poster board
- scissors
- glue or tape
- crayons, markers, or colored pencils

Directions

1. Copy the raven onto cardstock or poster board.
2. Color the raven black with an orange beak.
3. Cut out the raven and the cards.
4. Cut slits in the raven's wings to hold the Bible verse cards.
5. Choose one of the verses to memorize. Place the card on the bird holder after you have studied it.
6. To make a stand, cut a 3" x 12" strip of cardstock paper. Fold the strip in half and glue or tape the bird to the front of the stand.

Finished Product

Cut. Cut.

#7061 Bible Stories & Crafts: Animals ©Teacher Created Resources

Elijah and the Ravens

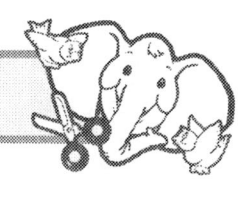

Craft: Bible Verse Raven *(cont.)*

Feed on God's Word!

The Lord will guide you always.

(Isaiah 58:11a)

Feed on God's Word!

Ask and it will be given to you; seek and you will find; knock and the door will be opened to you.

(Matthew 7:7)

Feed on God's Word!

I can do everything through him who gives me strength.

(Philippians 4:13)

Feed on God's Word!

I will hasten and not delay to obey your commands.

(Psalm 119:60)

Feed on God's Word!

Love is patient, love is kind. It does not envy, it does not boast, it is not proud.

(1 Corinthians 13:4)

Feed on God's Word!

I will instruct you and teach you in the way you should go.

(Psalm 32:8a)

Feed on God's Word!

And we know that in all things God works for the good of those who love him.

(Romans 8:28a)

Feed on God's Word!

God is light; in him there is no darkness at all.

(1 John 1:5b)

Elijah and the Ravens

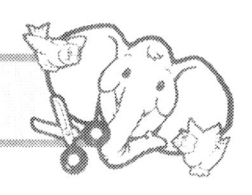

Craft: Flying Raven

Materials

- patterns on pages 64 and 65
- cardstock or poster board
- crayons, markers, or colored pencils
- heavy cardboard
- glue or tape
- scissors

Finished Product

Directions

1. Copy the raven pattern onto cardstock or poster board.
2. Color the raven and cut it out.
3. Fold the wings down on the dashed lines.
4. Cut a handle from heavy cardboard or copy the handle pattern below on heavy cardstock.
5. Glue or tape the handle to the back side of the raven.
6. Fly the raven through the air as you say the rhyme located on the front of the raven.

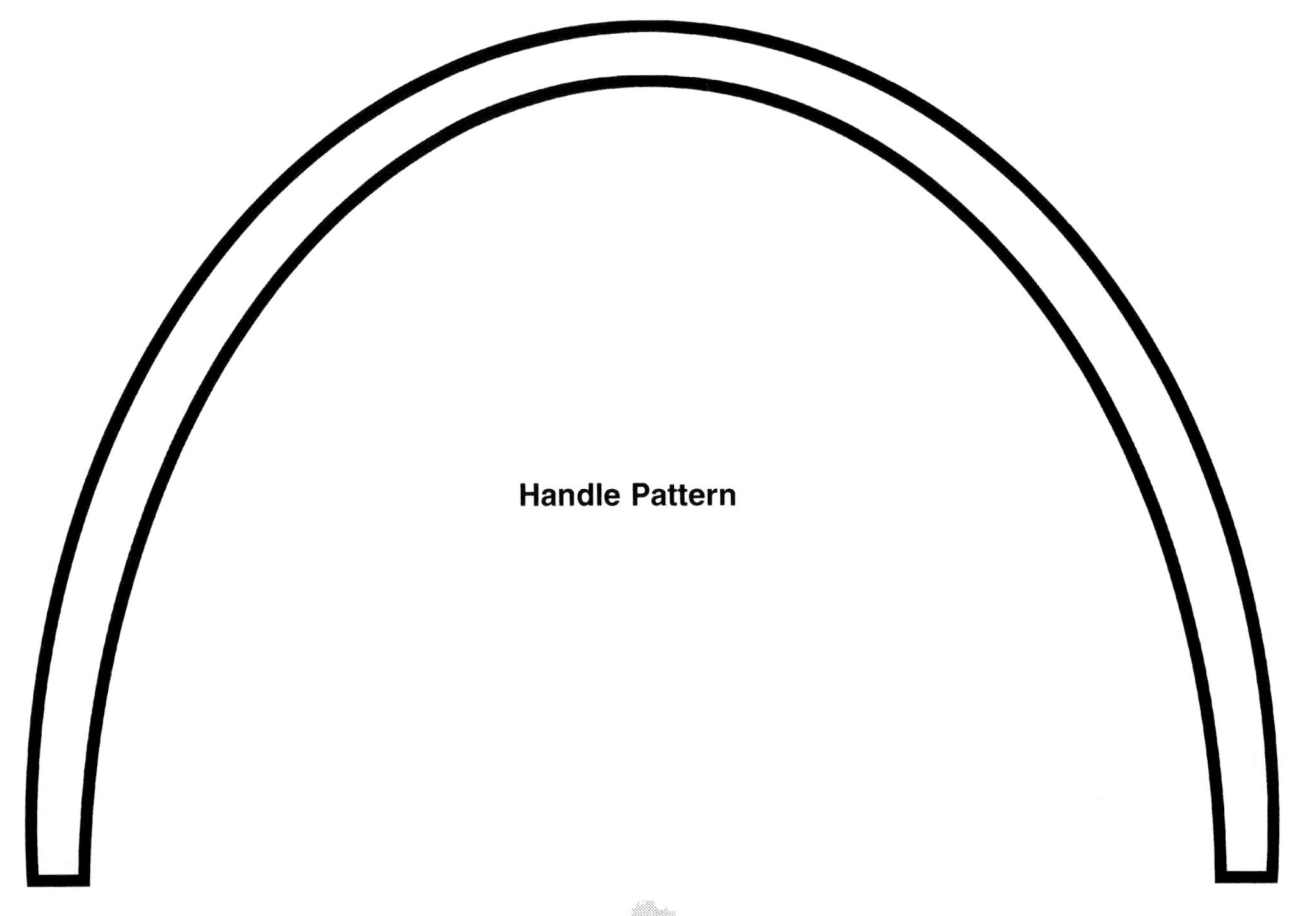

Handle Pattern

Elijah and the Ravens

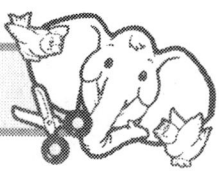

Craft: Flying Raven *(cont.)*
See page 64 for directions.

Fly, raven, fly—
Across the sunny sky.
Twice a day you head
To take Elijah bread.
He'll be so glad you came,
He'll praise God's holy name.

©Teacher Created Resources #7061 Bible Stories & Crafts: Animals

Balaam and His Donkey

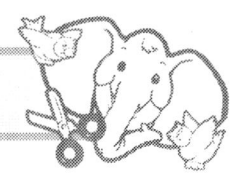

Bible Story: Numbers 22

Act out the story as you tell it to make it come alive for your students.

The Israelites were camped in Moab (on their way out of Egypt to the Promised Land). The king of Moab had heard what success the Israelites had in battle, so he joined forces with the Midianites to fight them. He was not sure what to do next, so he sent a message to Balaam (*point far away*).

Balaam was a prophet. He did not follow God, but he recognized that his special powers came from God. He was more concerned about himself than about pleasing God. When the messengers arrived at Balaam's house, they told him King Balak wanted him to come and put a curse on the Israelites so they could be defeated (*point to yourself and look surprised*). Balaam asked them to spend the night to give him time to decide what to do.

Balaam wanted to accept the money the king had sent for cursing the Israelites, but he knew a little about God, and putting a curse on God's chosen people did not sound like a wise thing to do. God spoke to Balaam that night: "Do not go with them. You must not put a curse on those people, because they are blessed." The next morning Balaam sent the messengers away without him (*wave goodbye*).

When the messengers returned to the king and gave him Balaam's answer, he decided Balaam needed more persuasion. He sent more messengers to tell him, "Do not let anything keep you from coming to me, because I will reward you handsomely and do whatever you say."

Balaam invited the messengers to stay at his house overnight while he waited to see what God would tell him. That night God spoke to Balaam again. "Since these men have come to summon you," God said, "go with them, but do only what I tell you." Balaam saddled his donkey the next morning and headed out (*walk around slowly as if riding a donkey*). God was angry with Balaam for being so greedy. He knew the prophet did not care about pleasing God; he just wanted his reward from the king. The angel of the Lord stood in the road to stop Balaam. He did not see Him, but his donkey did. When the donkey saw the angel of the Lord with a drawn sword in His hand, she turned off the road and went into a field. Balaam cruelly beat the donkey to get her back on the road (*smack leg*). As Balaam rode between two walled vineyards, the angel of the Lord stood in the narrow path. The donkey pressed close to the wall to avoid Him and Balaam's foot was crushed. (*howl in pain and smack leg twice*) He beat the donkey again. The angel of the Lord moved ahead and stood in the middle of the road in a place where the donkey could not go around Him. When the donkey saw Him again, she lay down and would not get up. Balaam was so angry he beat the donkey with his staff (*smack leg three times angrily*).

The Lord gave the donkey the power of speech and she said, "What have I done to you to make you beat me these three times." Balaam told the donkey that if he had had a sword he would kill her!" He was so angry, he did not even think about how strange a talking donkey was! (*Threaten angrily with a fist.*) Then the Lord opened Balaam's eyes and he saw the angel of the Lord in the road. Frightened, Balaam bowed in the road with his face down (*bow down*). The angel of the Lord pointed out that the donkey had saved Balaam's life. If the donkey had turned away, the angel would have killed him! He ordered Balaam to go ahead, but to speak only what God told him.

Balaam was only able to speak blessings on the Israelites, not curses (*cover mouth with hand*). It was not what King Balak wanted to hear, but God was controlling what Balaam said and the king could do nothing about it.

Balaam and His Donkey

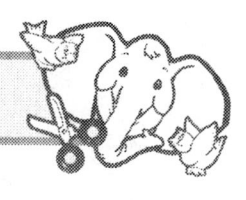

Discussion

- What does this story teach us about God?
- If God can use a donkey to do His will, He can certainly use you and me. How do you think He wants to use you? Are you willing for Him to use you?

Bible Verse

"My mouth will speak in praise of the Lord. Let every creature praise his holy name for ever and ever." (Psalm 145:21)

How can you speak in praise of the Lord everyday, no matter where you are?

Puppet Skit

Follow the directions on page 68 to make paper plate puppets. Let children hold them up as they act out the skit. Choose one to be Balaam while the others are donkeys and you read the angel's part. The children can make clip-clop sounds with their tongues or feet when the donkey is traveling.

Balaam:	Time to saddle my donkey and be off. I can hardly wait to see King Balak and get the money he promised me. I know God said He does not want me to curse His people, but maybe I can figure out a way around it. Come on, donkey, let's go.
Donkey:	Hee-Haw! Hee-Haw! (*clip-clop sounds*)
Balaam:	Why are you getting off the road? Whoa! Stop! I do not want to go into this field. Take that, you stupid donkey! (*slap hands together*)
Donkey:	Hee-Haw! Hee-Haw! (*as if in pain*)
Balaam:	That's better. Now just stay on this road and do what you are supposed to do. Wait a minute! Not so close to the wall! Ow! You crushed my foot, you dumb beast! Take that and that! (*slap hands together twice*) What is wrong with you today? You almost broke my foot!
Donkey:	(*clip-clop sounds*)
Balaam:	Now what? Why are you lying down? Get up! Get up! (*slap hands together*)
Donkey:	Why do you keep beating me? I haven't done anything wrong.
Balaam:	You stupid animal, if I had a sword I would kill you!
Angel:	Balaam, your donkey saved your life! If she hadn't stopped, I would have struck you down.
Balaam:	(*bowing down*) Oh no! Have mercy on me!

©Teacher Created Resources — #7061 *Bible Stories & Crafts: Animals*

Balaam and His Donkey

Craft: Donkey Paper Plate Puppet

Materials

- pattern below
- paper plate
- white paper
- scissors
- crayons or colored markers
- glue

Directions

1. Copy the donkey pattern onto white paper for children to color.
2. Cut out the pattern and glue it to a paper plate.
3. Hold the donkey face in front of your face.

Finished Product

Balaam and His Donkey

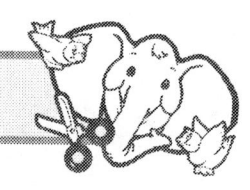

Craft: Donkey Wall Hanging

Materials

- pattern below
- cardstock or poster board
- clear adhesive plastic
- crayons, markers, or colored pencils
- ribbon or raffia *(optional)*
- wire
- scissors
- hole punch

Finished Product

Directions

1. Copy the pattern onto cardstock or poster board.
2. Color the pattern.
3. Cover the pattern with clear adhesive plastic to protect it and then cut it out.
4. Punch two holes in the top of the pattern with a hole punch.
5. Attach a wire in the holes for a hanger.
6. As an option, decorate the hanger with a bow of ribbon or raffia.

Nothing is impossible for God!

Just ask Balaam's donkey.

©Teacher Created Resources   #7061 Bible Stories & Crafts: Animals

Balaam and His Donkey

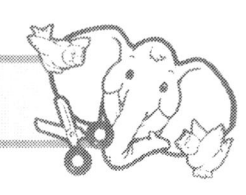

Craft: Donkey Bible Verse Reminder

Materials

- patterns on pages 70 and 71
- cardstock or poster board
- crayons, markers, or colored pencils
- scissors
- glue or tape

Directions

1. Copy the patterns onto cardstock or poster board.
2. Color the patterns and cut them out.
3. Glue or tape the mouth to the back of the head.
4. Lift the head to read the verse.

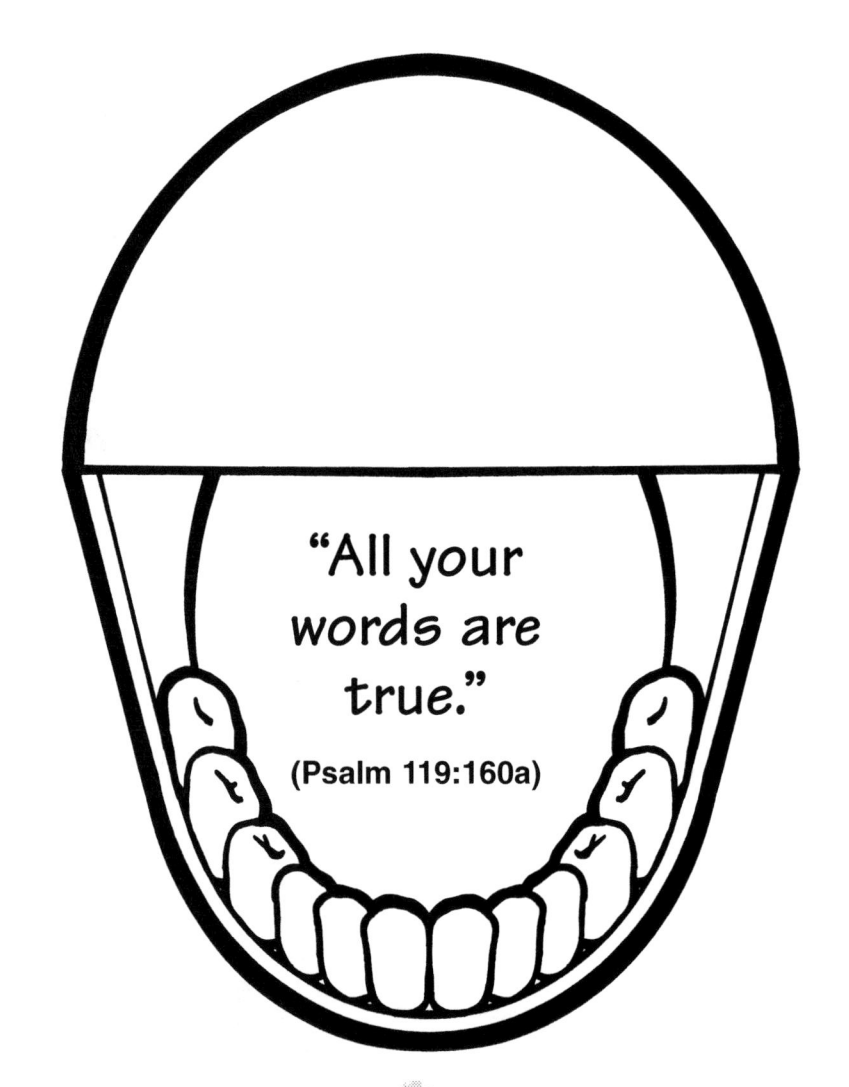

Finished Product

"All your words are true."

(Psalm 119:160a)

#7061 Bible Stories & Crafts: Animals ©Teacher Created Resources

Balaam and His Donkey

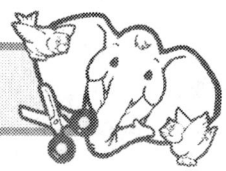

Craft: Donkey Bible Verse Reminder *(cont.)*

See page 70 for directions.

©Teacher Created Resources · #7061 Bible Stories & Crafts: Animals

God Talks to Job

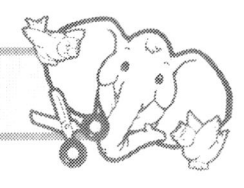

Bible Story: Job 39:13-18

As you tell what God said to Job about the ostrich, sketch one on the board, one part at a time as shown. Encourage students to make their own ostrich drawings as you talk.

Job was suffering from the death of his children, the loss of his possessions, and sores all over his body. He was discouraged and had started to question God. Why was God doing this to him? Job did not think he deserved what was happening to him. Could he really trust God to know best? Job's friends accused him of being sinful. They said God was punishing him for doing wrong. Job kept insisting that he had done nothing wrong. He just wished God would explain why He was doing what He was doing.

Finally, God spoke to Job, but He did not explain Himself. He did not promise to take away Job's troubles or heal his body. Instead, God pointed out His greatness and power. He reminded Job that He had created everything and kept it going. He talked about the amazing animals He had created. God said, "The wings of the ostrich flap joyfully, but they cannot compare with the pinions and feathers of the stork." The ostrich is the largest bird God created. It can weigh up to 300 pounds and be seven or eight feet tall. But for its size, its wings are small and useless for flying. It has to stay on the ground and just watch other birds fly. God also told Job, "She lays her eggs on the ground and lets them warm in the sand, unmindful that a foot may crush them, that some wild animal may trample them. She treats her young harshly, as if they were not hers; she cares not that her labor was in vain, for God did not endow her with wisdom or give her a share of good sense." Most birds are very careful of their eggs. They prepare comfortable nests in which to lay them, then protect them with their own feathered bodies. The ostrich lays her three-pound eggs in a nest with lots of eggs from other ostrich mothers. If there is no room left in the nest, she lays them somewhere in the sand where they lie unprotected. The eggs are often crushed by the ostrich hens getting in and out of the nest but the ostrich mother does not seem to care. She may act as if she does not even remember that the eggs are hers! Sometimes an ostrich becomes impatient and leaves the nest before the eggs hatch, or she may sit on another ostrich's eggs, as if she cannot remember which ones are hers. But God also pointed out to Job that though the ostrich was careless and not very bright, it could run like a horse, which no other bird could do.

Why did God talk about ostriches when Job was feeling discouraged? God wanted to remind him that the Creator of all things always knows what He is doing. He has a purpose for everything even though we may not understand it. Why would God create a bizarre bird like the ostrich? It was not Job's job to figure out why, anymore than it was his job to figure out why God was allowing him to suffer. The important thing was for Job to realize that God knows best and to trust Him.

Did Job get God's message? Yes. Job answered God, "I know that you can do all things; no plan of yours can be thwarted . . . My ears had heard of you but now my eyes have seen you." (Job 42:2, 5) Job trusted God through all his troubles, and God rewarded him by healing him and giving him far more than he had had before.

God Talks to Job

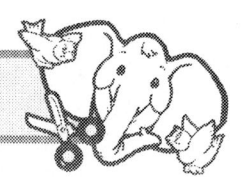

Dicussion

- What do ostriches teach us about God?
- Do you think God has a sense of humor? Why?

Bible Verse

"Stop and consider God's wonders." (Job 37:14b)

Do you think the ostrich is one of God's wonders? What are some others? What is God's greatest wonder?

Puppet Skit

Follow the directions on page 74 to make a walking ostrich puppet. Let students "walk" their puppets around as they sing the following song with you.

(*Tune:* "Did You Ever See a Lassie?")

Did you ever see an ostrich, an ostrich, an ostrich,

Did you ever see an ostrich run fast as a horse?

Run this way and that way, run that way and this way?

Did you ever see an ostrich run fast as a horse?

Did you know that God created, created, created,

Did you know that God created the ostrich Himself?

He made it so big and so fast and so silly.

Did you know that God created the ostrich Himself?

Did you know that God created, created, created,

Did you know that God created, created you too?

He made you and loves you and always cares for you.

Did you know that God created, created you too?

God Talks to Job

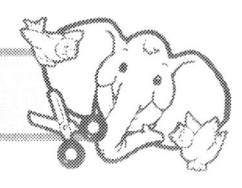

Craft: Walking Ostrich Puppet

Materials

- pattern below
- crayons or colored markers
- cardstock
- scissors

Directions

1. Copy the ostrich pattern onto cardstock for children to color.
2. Cut out the pattern.
3. Cut out the two holes at the bottom of the ostrich pattern. Make sure your first two fingers fit into the holes over the knuckles. Enlarge the holes as needed for a good fit. (*Caution:* Sharp pointed scissors are needed to cut out the holes, so a teacher should do the cutting for younger children.)
4. Fit the ostrich pattern on your hand, sticking your first two fingers through the holes to be the ostrich's legs. Move your fingers along the table to make the ostrich walk.

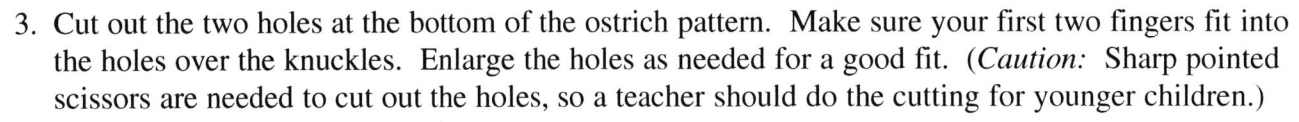

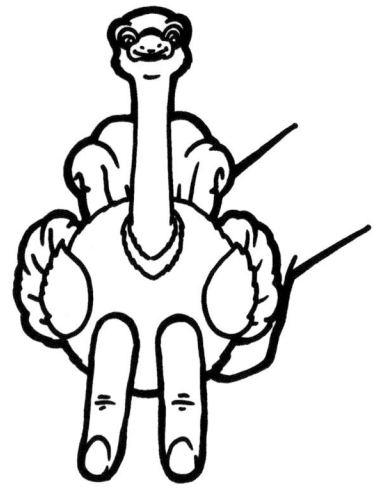

Finished Product

#7061 Bible Stories & Crafts: Animals   74   ©Teacher Created Resources

God Talks to Job

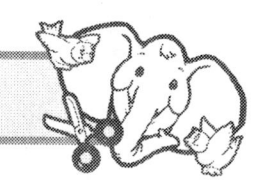

Craft: Paper Plate Ostrich

Materials

- patterns on pages 75 and 76
- cardstock or poster board
- crayons, markers, or colored pencils
- small paper plate
- scissors
- glue

Directions

1. Copy the patterns onto cardstock or poster board.
2. Color the patterns and cut them out.
3. Glue the patterns to a small paper plate to make an ostrich as shown. For the wing, place glue on the right hand side, so the wing is able to flap and you can see the poem.
4. Cut out the poem and glue it to the ostrich under the wing.

Finished Product

Look at the ostrich and wonder why
God gave her wings, but she can't fly.
Not very wise, common sense—she has none.
But me-oh-my! Just watch her run!

Head Pattern

©Teacher Created Resources #7061 Bible Stories & Crafts: Animals

God Talks to Job

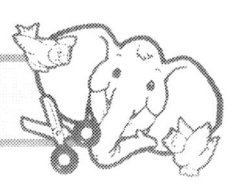

Craft: Paper Plate Ostrich *(cont.)*

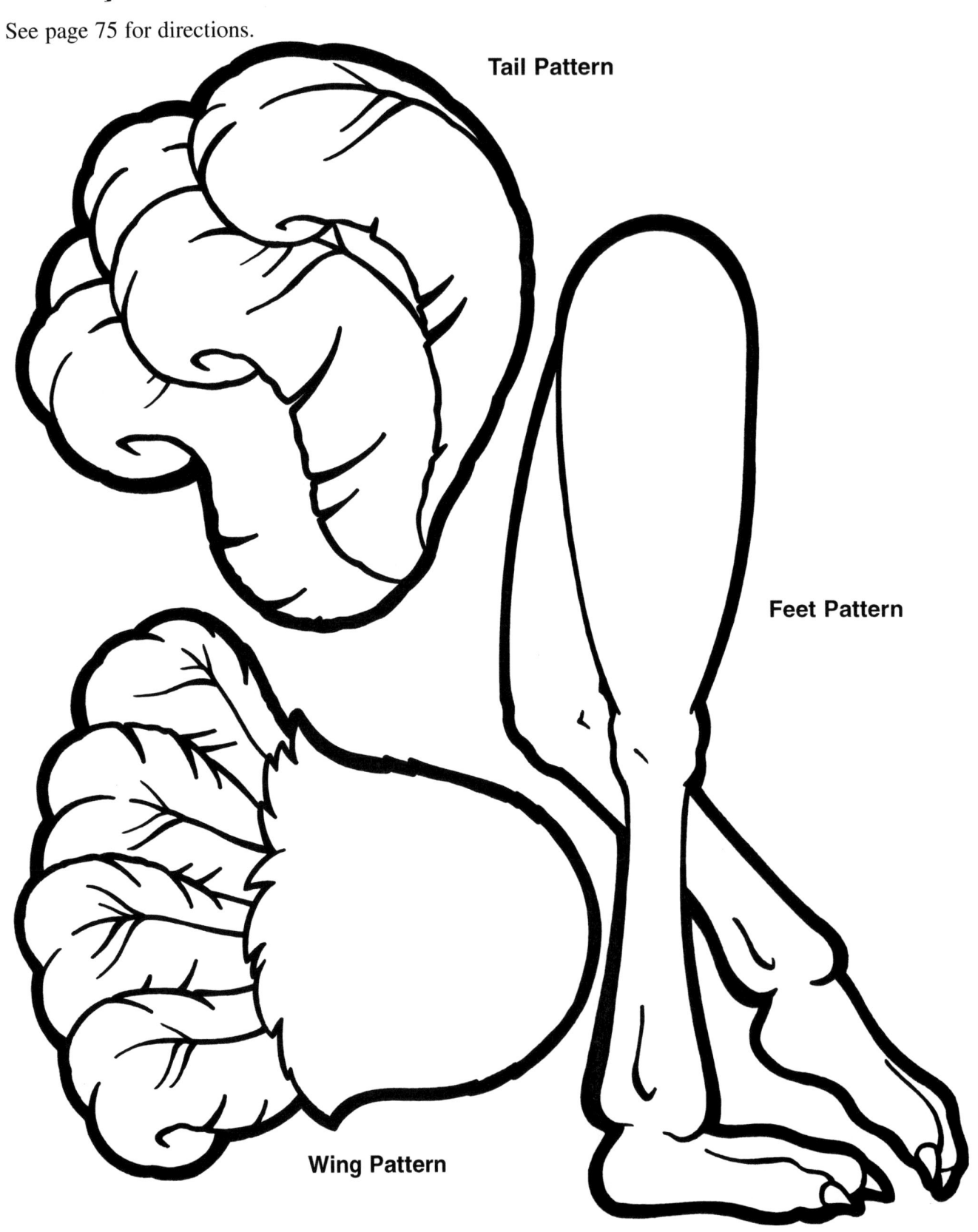

See page 75 for directions.

Tail Pattern

Feet Pattern

Wing Pattern

God Talks to Job

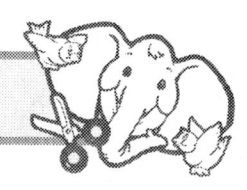

Craft: Ostrich Booklet

Materials

- patterns on pages 77 and 78
- construction paper
- white paper
- crayons, markers, or colored pencils
- scissors
- stapler and staples

Directions

1. Copy the pages below onto construction paper.
2. Copy page 78 on white paper.
3. Color the pages and cut them out.
4. Put the pages in order with the construction paper ones on the outside. (*Note:* The pages should be in the order of the spelling of "OSTRICH.") Staple them together on the left side.

Finished Product

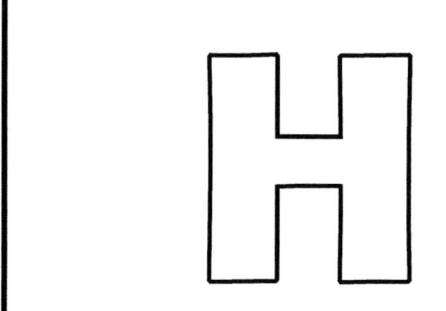

H

**Heaviest bird—
it can weigh 345 pounds!**

A Very Unusual BIRD

God Talks to Job

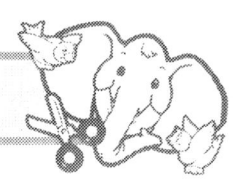

Craft: Ostrich Booklet *(cont.)*

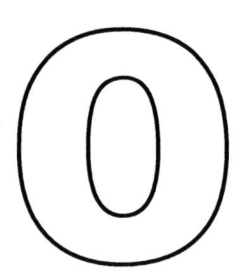

O — Offspring hatched from big eggs, about three pounds each!	**S** — Seeds, plants, and insects—favorite foods.
T — Tallest bird—up to nine feet tall!	**R** — Runs as fast as a horse!
I — Is not very wise—no common sense.	**C** — Created with wings, but cannot fly!

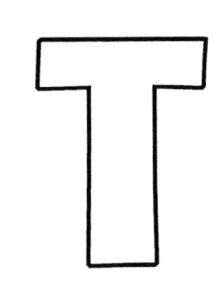

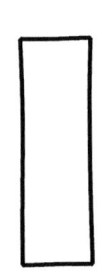

Daniel and the Lions

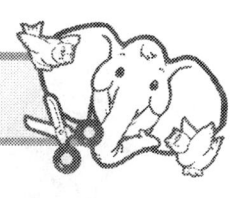

Bible Story: Daniel 6

Daniel's story is a familiar favorite of most children. Sing the story and have the children sing along.

(*Tune:* "Old MacDonald Had a Farm")

Daniel, Daniel, true to God, always did his best.

King Darius saw his work, and he was impressed.

But Daniel's enemies were mad, if they could trap him they'd be glad.

Daniel, Daniel, true to God, always did his best.

Daniel's enemies spoke up to the king and said,

"Anyone who breaks a law you make should be dead.

So make a law that prayer to you is all that everyone can do.

And any man who breaks the law to lions will be fed!

The law was made but Daniel paid no attention to it.

Three times a day he prayed to God 'cause it was right to do it.

King Darius sadly heard, but knew he couldn't break his word.

He had done a foolish thing, and Darius knew it.

The king had Daniel thrown into the hungry lions' den.

All night they prowled around, but that was not the end of him.

God sent an angel down to shut every lion's mouth right up.

Next day they lifted Daniel out and threw the bad guys in!

Daniel and the Lions

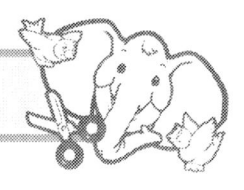

Discussion

How did Daniel prove that He loved God? How did Daniel's faith in God affect the king?

Bible Verse

"He rescues and he saves; he performs signs and wonders in the heavens and on the earth. He has rescued Daniel from the power of the lions." (Daniel 6:27)

Who spoke the words of this Bible verse? *(Read Daniel 6:26-27 to find out.)* Whom was he describing? Do you agree with his description? How has God rescued and saved you?

Puppet Skit

Follow the directions on page 81 to make face masks. Choose a child to be Daniel, and one to be King Darius. You be the narrator. The other children can be lions, using their face masks to act out this skit.

Narrator:	King Darius was pleased with Daniel and decided to give him an important job. Some of the king's other officials were jealous. They tried to bring charges against Daniel for some small wrongdoing so they could get rid of him; but Daniel was a godly man, and did nothing wrong! They came up with a plot to trick the king. They flattered him, telling him he was so great, no one should pray to anyone but him! They suggested he make a law that people could pray to no one but Darius for 30 days. Anyone who broke the law must be thrown to the lions. Foolishly, the king passed the law.
Daniel:	I know the king's new law says we must pray only to him, but I cannot do that. I have always prayed three times every day to God, and I will not stop now! *(Kneels down to pray)*
Narrator:	As soon as Daniel's enemies saw him praying, they reported him to the king and reminded Darius that he was breaking the law and must be punished.
King Darius:	Why did I ever make that stupid law! Well, I cannot change it now. Go arrest Daniel.
Narrator:	Daniel was thrown into the den of hungry lions.
Lions:	*(Prowling around Daniel, roaring and growling)*
Narrator:	The king worried all night and ran to the den the next morning to check on Daniel.
King Darius:	Daniel, are you there? Has your God saved you?
Daniel:	I'm fine! My God sent His angel to shut the mouths of the lions and keep me safe.
Lions:	*(Making noises with closed mouths)*

#7061 Bible Stories & Crafts: Animals   ©Teacher Created Resources

Daniel and the Lions

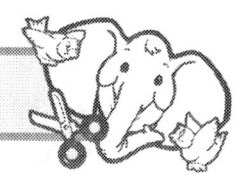

Craft: Lion Mask

Materials

- pattern below
- cardstock
- scissors
- crayons or colored markers
- hole punch
- string

Directions

1. Copy the lion mask onto cardstock.
2. Color the mask, then cut it out.
3. Punch a hole on each end of the mask.
4. Tie string in the holes.
5. Put the mask over your face and tie the string at the back of your head.

Finished Product

Daniel and the Lions

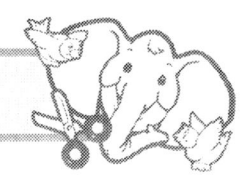

Craft: Lion Refrigerator Magnet

Materials

- pattern below
- cardstock or poster board
- crayons, markers, or colored pencils
- scissors
- magnet
- tan or brown tissue paper
- glue

Directions

1. Copy the pattern onto cardstock or poster board.
2. Color the pattern and cut it out.
3. Cut the tan or brown tissue paper into 1" squares. Squish them into small balls and glue them around the lion's mane.
4. Glue a magnet to the back to make a refrigerator decoration.

Don't be afraid whatever you do. As God protected Daniel, He will watch over you!

Finished Product

Daniel and the Lions

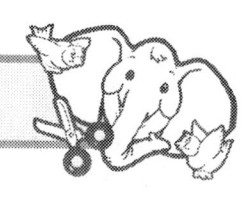

Craft: Stand-Up Lion

Materials

- patterns on pages 83 and 84
- cardstock or poster board
- crayons, markers, or colored pencils
- tape
- scissors
- glue

Directions

1. Copy the patterns onto cardstock or poster board.
2. Color the patterns and cut them out.
3. Fold the body of the lion in half.
4. Glue or tape the lion's heads onto both sides.
5. Tape the top of the lion's body together.
6. Slightly fold out the feet so that the lion is standing up.

Finished Product

©Teacher Created Resources #7061 Bible Stories & Crafts: Animals

Daniel and the Lions

Craft: Stand-Up Lion *(cont.)*

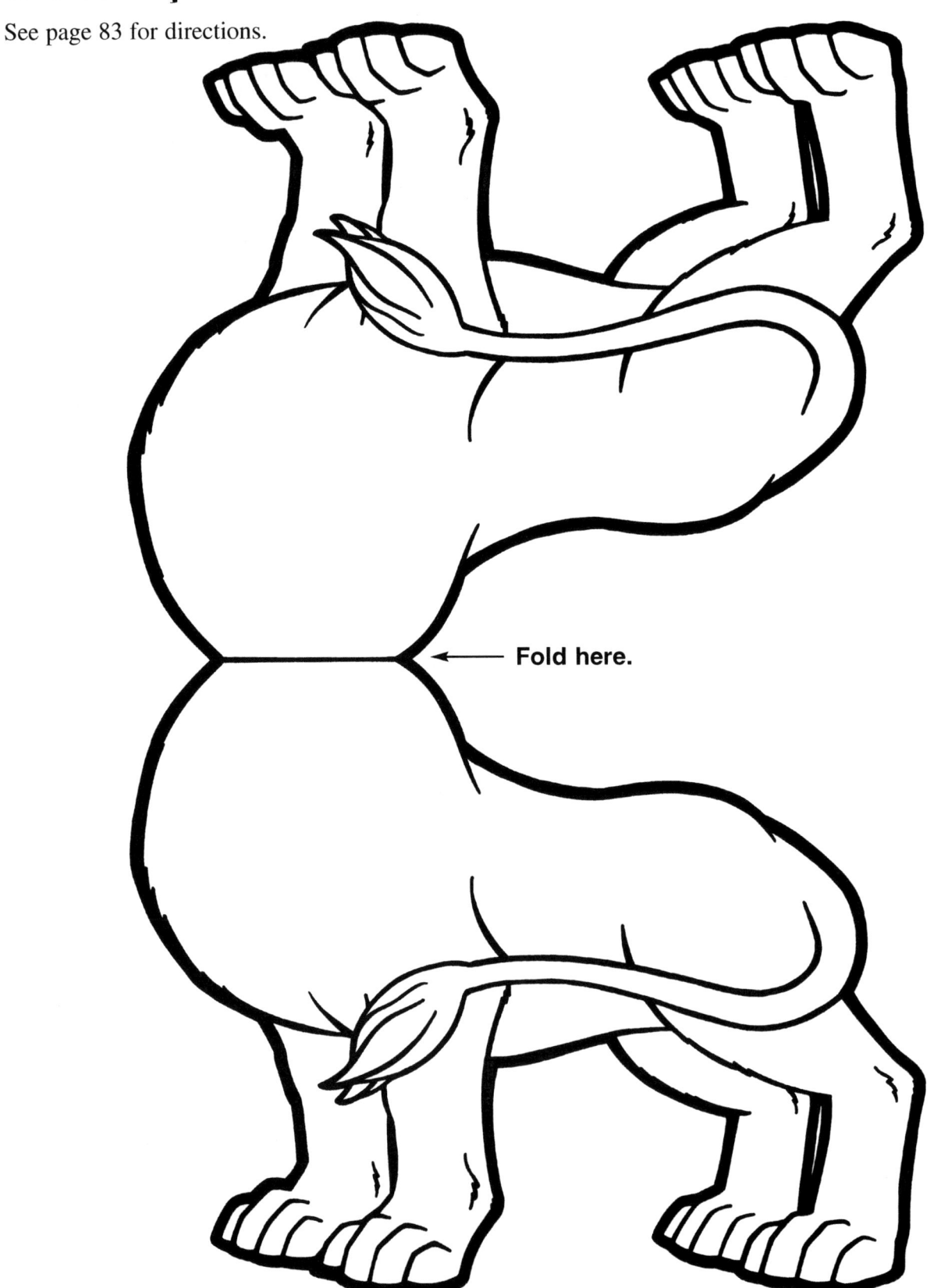

See page 83 for directions.

← Fold here.

#7061 *Bible Stories & Crafts: Animals*   84   ©*Teacher Created Resources*

Jonah and the Great Fish

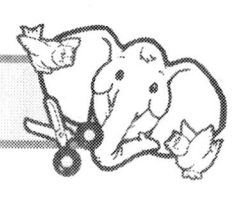

Bible Story: Jonah 1-2

Arrange children's chairs in a boat shape or have them sit on the floor as if they are on a boat. Draw a whale shape with an open mouth on a large sheet of cardboard. Lean the cardboard against a table (you may want to tape it to the table legs to secure it). At the appropriate time in the story, children can take turns jumping out of the boat, "swimming" around, and going "into" the whale's mouth.

Jonah was on a boat. Why? He was trying to run away from God! He didn't want to do what God had told him to do, so Jonah got on a boat headed for Tarshish. It was not that he had always wanted to take a voyage to Tarshish; it is just that it was in the exact opposite direction of Nineveh, where God had told him to go. Of course, we all know you cannot run from God. Jonah soon found that out, too.

Jonah was taking a nap when the ship was hit by a terrible storm on the sea. The ship rocked back and forth and up and down in the crashing waves. (*Have children sway back and forth in their seats.*) The storm was hitting the ship so hard, the experienced sailors thought it would break apart and they would all drown. They were crying out in fear to their gods. They began throwing the ship's cargo overboard to lighten the ship. Maybe that would help. (*Let children pretend to throw things overboard.*) But it didn't. The captain went down where Jonah was sleeping and woke him up to tell him what was happening. He could not believe Jonah could be calmly sleeping in the middle of such a storm. He told Jonah to get up and pray to his God that they would not all be drowned.

Some of the sailors decided to cast lots to see if they could find out whose fault the storm was. Casting lots was a little bit like throwing dice. Somehow, the lots showed that Jonah was the problem. The sailors questioned him and Jonah told them that he worshiped God, the Creator of the sea and the land. He explained that he was running away from the Lord. When they asked him what they should do, Jonah told them to throw him overboard. Nobody wanted to do that. Jonah would surely drown in such a stormy sea. The sailors tried to row the ship to land, but the sea grew even wilder! Finally, they decided if they wanted to survive, Jonah would have to go. They picked him up and threw him over the side of the ship into the sea. (*Let children pretend to throw a classmember overboard.*)

Immediately, the stormy sea calmed down. The ship stopped tossing and the captain and sailors were safe. But what about Jonah? Did he drown in the sea? (*The child thrown overboard pretends to swim.*) Amazingly, Jonah did not drown. God sent along a big fish to swallow him whole! (*The child should "swim" into the cardboard fish.*) Inside the fish, Jonah was wet and frightened, but alive. He had learned his lesson. He stopped rebelling against God and began praying. For three days and nights Jonah was in the fish's belly. Then one day God made the fish spit Jonah out, not in the middle of the sea, but on dry ground! (*Have the child walk out from under the table.*)

God told Jonah again to go to Nineveh to preach to the people, and this time Jonah obeyed. He hurried off toward Nineveh, glad to leave his "fishy" experience behind him. Jonah had learned that when God tells you what to do, you'd better do it because He has interesting ways of convincing you.

Jonah and the Great Fish

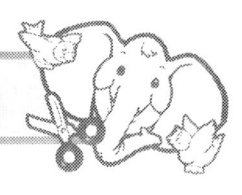

Discussion

- What do you think the sailors thought when they saw the fish swallow Jonah?
- Why do you think God made Jonah stay inside the fish for three days and nights?
- How did the fish prove God's love for Jonah?

Bible Verse

". . . In my distress I called to the Lord, and he answered me." (Jonah 2:2a)

What is the best thing to do when you are in trouble? How has the Lord helped you when you were in trouble?

Puppet Skit

Follow the directions on page 87 to make hand puppets. Let children use the puppets to act out the following rhyming skit.

> Jonah sailing in a ship far across the sea,
>
> *(Rock Jonah puppet back and forth.)*
>
> Trying hard to run from God, thinking God won't see.
>
> *(Keep rocking Jonah puppet.)*
>
> Suddenly a storm comes up and sailors start to pray.
>
> *(Rock Jonah puppet harder.)*
>
> They throw Jonah overboard; it's the only way.
>
> *(Move hand down so Jonah puppet slowly sinks.)*
>
> Instantly the sea is calm, then with a slurpy swish,
>
> *(Move fish puppet under Jonah and "swallow" the Jonah puppet.)*
>
> Jonah ends up in the belly of a giant fish!
>
> *(Hold Jonah puppet in fish puppet's mouth.)*
>
> Jonah prays to God as the fish swims slowly 'round,
>
> *("Swim" the fish puppet around with the Jonah puppet inside.)*
>
> Three days later it spits Jonah out on the dry ground.
>
> *(Remove the Jonah puppet and "swim" the fish puppet away.)*

Jonah and the Great Fish

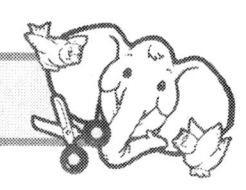

Craft: Great Fish Hand Puppet

Materials

- patterns below
- cardstock
- crayons or colored markers
- scissors
- small envelope
- transparent tape
- glue

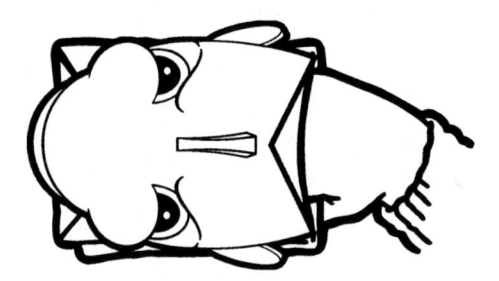

Finished Product

Directions

1. Copy the patterns onto cardstock and color them. Cut the patterns out.
2. Glue the tabs of the Jonah puppet together at the back to fit your finger.
3. Fold the envelope in half, then carefully cut through the top layer at the folded edge. Keep it attached at the bottom, so you can slip your fingers in the top half and your thumb in the bottom half.
4. Tape the open edges of the envelope closed where needed so it stays on your hand.
5. Glue the fish pattern on the top of the envelope. On the inside, color a pink tongue.
6. Use the Jonah finger puppet with the fish hand puppet to act out the story of Jonah.

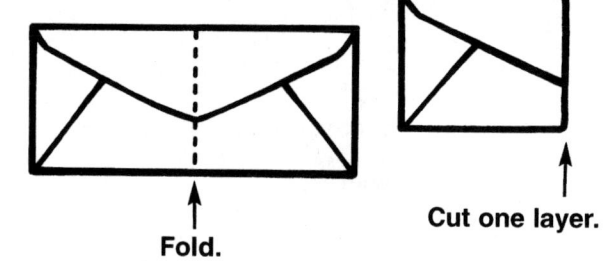

Fold.

Cut one layer.

Fish Pattern

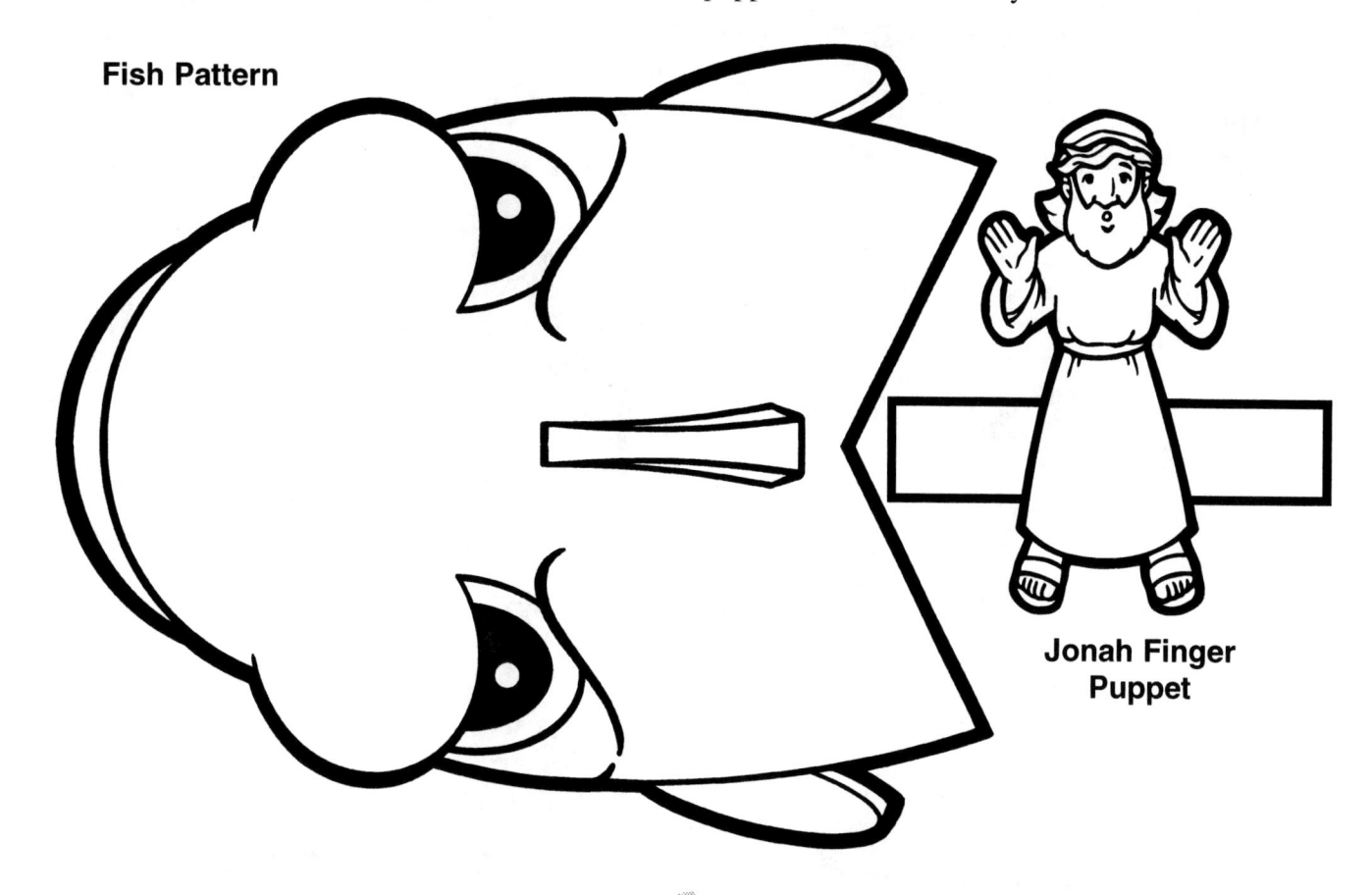

Jonah Finger Puppet

©Teacher Created Resources   #7061 Bible Stories & Crafts: Animals

Jonah and the Great Fish

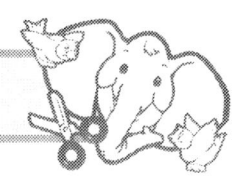

Craft: Switch Plate Cover

Materials

- patterns below
- cardstock or poster board
- crayons, markers, or colored pencils
- clear adhesive plastic *(optional)*
- glue
- scissors
- tape or sticky-tack

Finished Product

Directions

1. Copy the patterns onto cardstock or poster board.
2. Color the patterns.
3. Use clear adhesive plastic to cover the patterns and protect them.
4. Cut out the patterns.
5. Cut out the rectangle in the center of the switch plate cover.
6. Glue the sun to the top of the switch plate cover as shown.
7. Use sticky-tack or tape to cover your switch plate with the pattern.

#7061 Bible Stories & Crafts: Animals © Teacher Created Resources

Jonah and the Great Fish

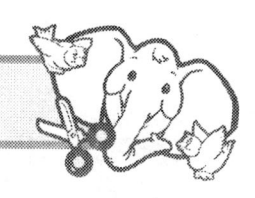

Craft: Jonah Mobile

Materials

- patterns on pages 89–91
- cardstock or poster board
- crayons, markers, or colored pencils
- string or yarn
- scissors
- hole punch

Directions

1. Copy the patterns onto cardstock or poster board.
2. Color the patterns.
3. Cut out the patterns. Use a hole punch to punch a hole in each one of the small patterns. Then punch the seven holes located on the boat pattern.
4. Attach the small pieces to the boat pattern with string or yarn as shown.
5. Tie 15" to 18" piece of string to the top of the boat pattern as shown for a hanger.

Finished Product

©Teacher Created Resources #7061 Bible Stories & Crafts: Animals

Jonah and the Great Fish

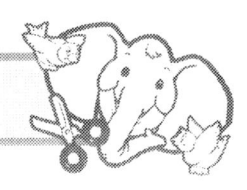

Craft: Jonah Mobile *(cont.)*

See page 89 for directions.

#7061 Bible Stories & Crafts: Animals ©Teacher Created Resources

Jonah and the Great Fish

Craft: Jonah Mobile *(cont.)*

See page 89 for directions.

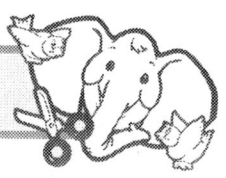

Boat Pattern

You can't run from God – He knows where you are!

©Teacher Created Resources 91 #7061 Bible Stories & Crafts: Animals

Baby Jesus and Animals

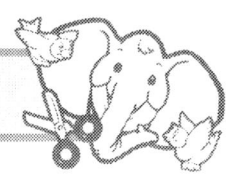

Bible Story: Luke 2:1-20; Matthew 2:1-12

As you tell this familiar Bible story, ask questions so children can supply the facts they know and express their ideas.

The town of Bethlehem was noisy and crowded when Mary and Joseph finally arrived. It was not exactly where they wanted to be with Mary ready to give birth to a baby anytime now, but they had no choice. Why did they have to be in Bethlehem? (*Let children answer that they were obeying a royal decree for everyone to go to register to be taxed in their hometowns. Joseph's family was from Bethlehem.*) Since there were so many other people in town, the inn was full. Where did Mary and Joseph go to spend the night? (*Let children answer that they went to a stable where animals were kept.*) Of course, this was not a problem or a surprise to God. In fact, He had planned it all so that His Son would be born in Bethlehem.

That night Mary gave birth to a baby boy in the stable. What animals do you think were in the stable that night? (*Let children share their ideas.*) How did Mary and Joseph decide what to name her baby? (*Let children answer that the angel Gabriel had already told them the baby should be named Jesus.*) Where did Baby Jesus take His first nap? (*Let children answer that He slept in a manger.*) The stable animals must have looked in amazement at a baby sleeping in the manger from which they usually ate!

The first people to find out about Jesus' birth were shepherds watching over their flocks of sheep in fields near Bethlehem. How did they find out about Jesus' birth? (*Let children tell about the angel that appeared to the shepherds and told them a Savior had been born in Bethlehem.*) The shepherds were afraid when they first saw the angel, but they were thrilled to hear his message. After a sky full of angels praised God, they suddenly went away. The shepherds jumped up and headed for Bethlehem to find the baby. What did they do after they found Him? (*Let children tell how the shepherds told everyone what they had seen and glorified God.*)

A couple of years later when Jesus was about two years old, He had more visitors. Who came to see Him and brought Him gifts? (*Let children tell about the wise men who traveled from the east to find the King of the Jews.*) We do not know for sure how the wise men got to Israel, but they probably rode on camels. How did they know where to come? (*Let children tell about the star that guided them.*) The wise men did not go directly to Bethlehem. Where did they stop for directions? (*Let children explain how the wise men stopped in Jerusalem and asked King Herod how to find the baby, and he called for the chief priests and teachers. They found out by reading the Old Testament book of Micah that Jesus would be born in Bethlehem.*) The wise men traveled to Bethlehem and the star stopped right over the house where Jesus was. The wise men went in and gave Him their gifts. What were their gifts? (*Let children answer that their gifts were gold, incense, and myrrh.*)

In a dream, God warned the wise men not to go back home through Jerusalem because Herod would want to question them about where Jesus was. He had told them he wanted to worship Jesus, but he actually wanted to kill Him! But God was watching out for His Son and before Herod had a chance to harm Him, God told Joseph to take his family to Egypt where they would be safe.

Discussion

- How do you think Joseph cleaned up the messy stable?
- What did he and Mary probably use for a bed?

Baby Jesus and Animals

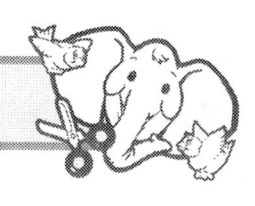

Bible Verse

"... at the name of Jesus every knee should bow, in heaven and on earth and under the earth." (Philippians 2:10)

Who bowed down and worshiped Jesus in our Bible story? How do you think the animals responded to Him? Animals do not think like people do, so they cannot worship Him. But they obey Him by following the instincts He gave them and doing what they are meant to do. That is a good example for us to follow!

Puppet Skit

Follow the directions on page 94 to make glove puppets. Let children use them to act out the following skit. Choose a good reader to read the part of each animal as the rest of the children manipulate that puppet on their gloves.

Cow: I woke up when some people came into my stable. It wasn't time to be fed or be let out. I wondered who they could be. It was a man and woman. She was going to have a baby—very soon.

Rooster: I was looking for bugs in the hay when the two people walked in. I had to fly up to a rafter to get out of the way. The man helped the woman lie down in the hay and held her hand.

Donkey: We all watched as the woman gave birth to a baby boy. She and the man looked so happy. They named Him Jesus.

Sheep: The woman laid her baby in the manger, where our master usually puts our food. But we did not mind sharing it. The baby needed a bed.

Rooster: Things were just settling down again when some noisy shepherds came in. They said an angel had told them God's Son had been born in a stable and they had come to see Him.

Cow: The Son of God, the One who made us all, was right there in our stable!

Sheep: One of the shepherds patted my head and told me that God's Word said this baby would grow up to be a special shepherd.

Rooster: None of us understood just what was happening, but we decided to announce Baby Jesus' birth ourselves. *(Children make animal sounds for the four animal puppets.)*

Camel: I saw Jesus later when He was living in a house with His parents. Two of my brothers and I brought our masters many, many miles to find God's Son and worship Him. I stayed outside, but I could tell when my master came back out that he had seen a miracle!

(Children make animal sounds for each of the animal puppets, including the camel.)

Baby Jesus and Animals

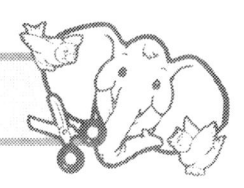

Craft: Animal Glove Puppets

Materials

- patterns below
- cardstock
- crayons, markers, or colored pencils
- pencils
- children's gloves (Have children bring old ones from home.)
- craft glue
- scissors

Directions

Finished Product

1. Copy the animal patterns onto cardstock and have children color them.

2. Help each child trace a hand, fingers slightly separated, on cardstock and cut it out.

3. Cut out the patterns and carefully glue one to each finger (and thumb) of the glove. In order to keep the glue from soaking through the gloves and sticking the fingers together, insert the cardstock hand shape into the glove before gluing the patterns on the fingers.

4. Let the glue dry completely. Then have children carefully remove the cardstock hand shape and put on their gloves. Have children wiggle their fingers to make the animal puppets move.

#7061 Bible Stories & Crafts: Animals ©Teacher Created Resources

Baby Jesus and Animals

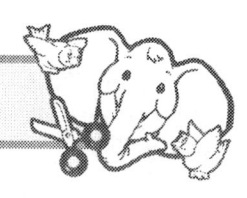

Craft: Fingerprint Animals

Materials

- pattern below
- construction paper
- colored markers
- scissors
- ink pad
- glue

Finished Product

Directions

1. Copy the pattern, color it, and cut it out.
2. Glue the pattern to a sheet of construction paper.
3. Add animals to the manger scene by making fingerprints in various places (one for small animals such as sheep, two for cows and donkeys).
4. Use markers to add legs, eyes, noses, and ears to the animals.

©Teacher Created Resources   #7061 Bible Stories & Crafts: Animals

Baby Jesus and Animals

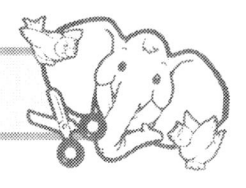

Craft: Camel Pop-Up Card

Materials

- patterns on pages 96–98
- cardstock or poster board
- crayons, markers, or colored pencils
- scissors
- white paper
- glue

Directions

1. Copy the card patterns back to back onto cardstock or poster board.
2. Copy the camel onto white paper and cut it out. Color the card and camel.
3. Fold the camel head in half. Place dots of glue on the Xs on the card. Firmly press the camel's ears and tassels on the glue. Make sure the folded edge pops out while gluing. Also, make sure the glue completely dries so the camel stays attached to the card.
4. Trim the edges off the card and fold it in the middle. When you open the card, the camel should pop out.

Finished Product

#7061 Bible Stories & Crafts: Animals ©Teacher Created Resources

Baby Jesus and Animals

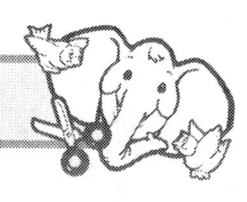

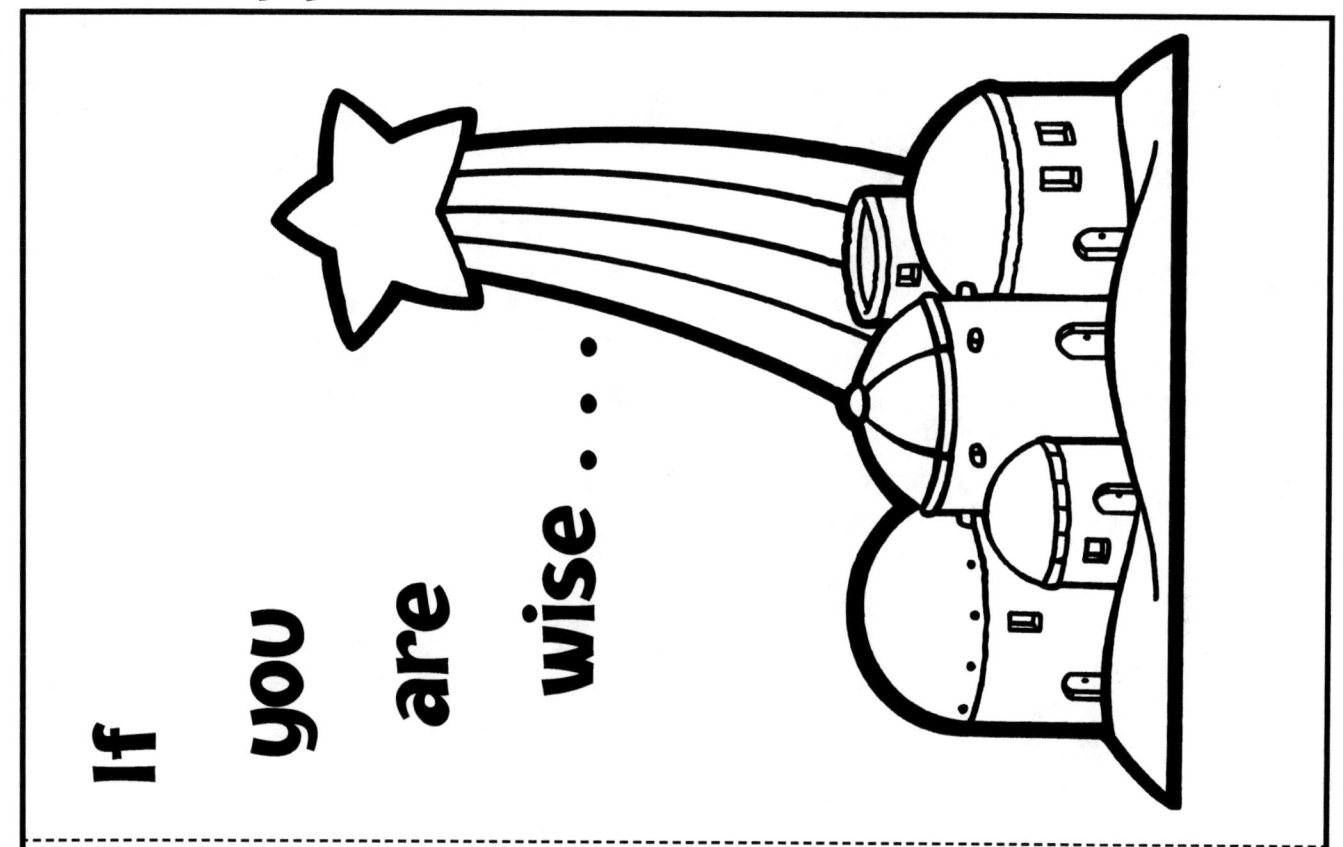

Craft: Camel Pop-Up Card *(cont.)*   Front of Card

If you are wise . . .

Baby Jesus and Animals

Craft: Camel Pop-Up Card *(cont.)*   Inside of Card

you will follow JESUS!

x   x

Wise men traveled from far away to find the Savior to worship that day.
(Matthew 2:1–11)

x   x

Jesus Is Baptized

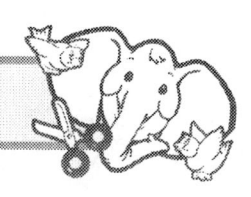

Bible Story: Matthew 3:13-17; John 1:29-34

Have children say each line of this Bible story echo rhyme after you.

Leader	**Echo**
Down by the river	Down by the river
John is preaching loud,	John is preaching loud,
Saying, "You must all repent!"	Saying, "You must all repent!"
To the listening crowd.	To the listening crowd.
Suddenly John looks up,	Suddenly John looks up,
Sees Jesus on His way,	Sees Jesus on His way,
And says, "Look, the Lamb of God	And says, "Look, the Lamb of God
Who takes our sins away!"	Who takes our sins away!"
Jesus wants to be baptized,	Jesus wants to be baptized,
So John takes His hand.	So John takes His hand.
They step into the water	They step into the water
And carry out God's plan.	And carry out God's plan.
Jesus looks up at the sky	Jesus looks up at the sky
And sees a flying dove.	And sees a flying dove.
It lands on Him as a sign	It lands on Him as a sign
Of His Father's love.	Of His Father's love.
The dove's the Holy Spirit,	The dove's the Holy Spirit,
And God speaks from above,	And God speaks from above,
"I am well pleased with Him,	"I am well pleased with Him,
This Son whom I love."	This Son whom I love."

©Teacher Created Resources   #7061 Bible Stories & Crafts: Animals

Jesus Is Baptized

Discussion

How do you think John felt about baptizing Jesus? Read Matthew 3:14 to find out.

Bible Verse

"The Spirit himself testifies with our spirit that we are God's children." (Romans 8:16)

What did the Holy Spirit show everyone about Jesus? What does the Holy Spirit do for us?

Puppet Skit

Follow the directions on page 101 to make a dove puppet. Let children use their puppets to act out the following skit. Choose three children to read the parts as the rest of the children "fly" their dove puppets around (but not too energetically).

Child 1:	When Jesus was baptized a dove flew down and settled on Him.
Child 2:	Wow! Why did it do that?
Child 3:	The dove was really the Holy Spirit, showing everyone that Jesus was God's Son.
Child 1:	Did you know that this fulfilled a prophecy made hundreds of years before Jesus was born?
Child 3:	Yes, the prophet Isaiah said, "The Spirit of the LORD will rest on him," when he described the Messiah.
Child 2:	And then God spoke from heaven, didn't he?
Child 1:	Yes, God told everyone that Jesus was His Son and He loved Him.
Child 3:	God also said that He was pleased with Jesus.
Child 2:	From now on, everytime I see a dove I'm going to think of the Holy Spirit.
Child 1:	That's a good idea! And remember that when we love Jesus, God's Holy Spirit lives in us.
Child 3:	No wonder the word DOVE rhymes with LOVE!

Jesus Is Baptized

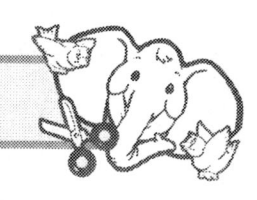

Craft: Dove Puppet

Materials

- pattern below
- white paper
- crayons or colored markers
- glue or tape
- craft stick
- scissors

Finished Product

Directions

1. Copy the dove pattern onto white paper.
2. Color the dove and then cut it out. (*Note:* Do not cut the body where the edges join together.)
3. Fold the dove in half down the center and fold the wings down so they flap.
4. Cut a slit at the bottom of the bird. Cut the slit big enough for the craft stick to slide through.
5. Slide the craft stick through the slit and attach by gluing or taping it to the dove. Then tape the body of the dove together.
6. "Fly" the dove by moving it up and down in the air as you move.

Fold here.

©Teacher Created Resources #7061 Bible Stories & Crafts: Animals

Jesus Is Baptized

Craft: Baptism Picture

Materials

- pattern below
- baptism picture on page 103
- white cardstock or poster board
- crayons, markers, or colored pencils
- scissors
- craft stick
- glue

Directions

1. Copy the pattern below and the picture onto white cardstock or poster board.
2. Color the dove pattern and cut it out.
3. Glue the dove to the end of a craft stick.
4. Color the baptism picture and cut it out.
5. Cut a slit in the picture from the cloud to the figure of Jesus.
6. From the back of the picture, insert the craft stick through the slit so the dove appears in the picture.
7. Move the dove down from the cloud to the figure of Jesus as it happened in the Bible story.

Finished Product

Jesus Is Baptized

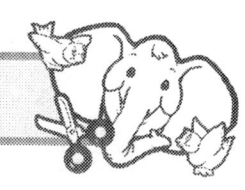

Craft: Baptism Picture *(cont.)*

©Teacher Created Resources · 103 · #7061 Bible Stories & Crafts: Animals

Jesus Is Baptized

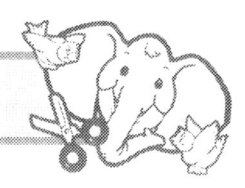

Craft: Dove Mobile

- pattern below and on page 105
- cardstock or poster board
- crayons, markers, or colored pencils
- cotton balls
- hole punch
- glitter
- glue
- scissors
- string

Directions

1. Copy the patterns onto white cardstock.
2. Color the dove and cut it out.
3. Trace the words with glue. Sprinkle glitter on the glue.
4. Cut out the cloud and glue cotton balls on it.
5. Use a 6- to 10-inch piece of string to tie the dove to the cloud.
6. Punch holes in the cloud, add string or yarn to make a loop, and hang your mobile.

Finished Product

Jesus Is Baptized

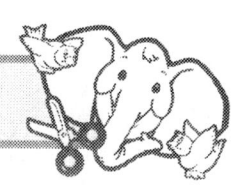

Craft: Dove Mobile *(cont.)*

©*Teacher Created Resources*   105   #7061 *Bible Stories & Crafts: Animals*

Jesus Deals with Demons

Bible Story: Mark 5:1-20

Choose an adult or a student who is a good reader to read the part of the pig farmer in this interview. You read the part of the interviewer. To make the news report more realistic, speak into a microphone (a real one or look-alike one you have made).

Interviewer: Hello, this is your on-the-street reporter for WKDZ, bringing you the latest news update. I am speaking today from the region of the Gerasenes, and I have an amazing story for you. I came here today after hearing about a miracle of healing performed by Jesus. This is the same Jesus who has claimed to be the Son of God. He has been teaching and healing people in many places, and it is hard to get near Him because of the crowds of people that have started following Him. I was not able to get an interview with Jesus, but we do have a special guest today. He is Joel, a local pig farmer. Thanks for talking with us, sir.

Pig Farmer: You're welcome.

Interviewer: Now, we have heard that Jesus came here by boat and when he walked ashore, a demon-possessed man went running to meet Him. Is that right?

Pig Farmer: Yes. We all thought the man was crazy. He lived in the tombs over there. They chained him up, but he always broke the chains. We were all scared to get too close to him; we didn't know what he might do.

Interviewer: What did Jesus do when the man ran up to Him?

Pig Farmer: The man begged Jesus to deliver him from the demons and Jesus agreed. The strange thing was that the demons inside the man spoke to Jesus. They begged Him not to send them away, but to put them in my herd of pigs that were over there on that hill.

Interviewer: And Jesus did what they asked?

Pig Farmer: Yes, but when the demons left the man and went into my pigs, my whole herd went crazy and ran down the hill right into the lake! All two thousand of them were drowned! It was scary, but it made me mad too!

Interviewer: Were all these people here when it happened?

Pig Farmer: No, some people who saw the miracle ran around telling people what had happened, so they all came to see for themselves. There wasn't much to see by the time they got here except the bodies of my pigs in the lake.

Interviewer: Where is the man who was healed?

Pig Farmer: That's him over there with Jesus. It is the first time I have ever seen him in his right mind, talking like a normal person. I heard him ask Jesus to take him along when He leaves, but Jesus told him to go home and tell what God had done for him.

Interviewer: Thanks for explaining what happened. Sorry about your pigs. That's our up-to-the-minute report here in the Gerasenes. Stay tuned to WKDZ for a full report later tonight.

Jesus Deals with Demons

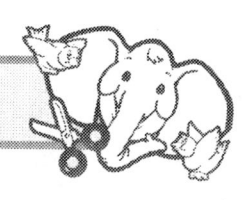

Discussion

The Bible tells us that the people who lived in the area of the Gerasenes begged Jesus to leave there. Why do you think they didn't want Him around? Why do you think Jesus told the healed man to go back home and tell what had happened to him instead of going with Him?

Bible Verse

"Therefore, if anyone is in Christ, he is a new creation; the old has gone, the new has come!"
(2 Corinthians 5:17)

How was the healed man a new creation after he met Jesus? What do you think he told his friends and family at home?

Puppet Skit

Follow the directions on page 108 to make a paper bag puppet. Let children use their puppets to act out the following skit. Let children read in pairs if you have a large group.

Pig 1:	(*Pig grunts*) Did you hear what happened to the pigs down the road yesterday?
Pig 2:	(*Pig grunts*) No! What happened?
Pig 3:	I heard; let me tell! (*Pig grunts*) A human named Jesus healed that man who had demons.
Pig 4:	You mean that crazy human who used to chase us? I was always afraid he would eat us if he caught us! (*Pig grunts*)
Pig 1:	Yes, that one. Jesus took the demons out of him.
Pig 5:	And he let the demons go into the herd of pigs that were on the hill.
Pig 2:	Oh no! (*Pig squeals*)
Pig 3:	The demons made the pigs go crazy. They ran down the hill into the lake!
Pig 2:	Were they hurt?
Pig 5:	All drowned. (*All pigs grunt and squeal*)
Pig 1:	But the human is fine now. He won't be chasing us anymore. He went home to tell everyone how Jesus healed him.
All Pigs:	Good for the humans, but bad for the pigs. (*Pig grunts*)

©Teacher Created Resources #7061 Bible Stories & Crafts: Animals

Jesus Deals with Demons

Craft: Pig Paper Bag Puppet

Materials

- patterns below
- white paper
- paper lunch bag
- crayons or colored markers
- scissors
- glue or glue stick

Directions

1. Copy the patterns below onto white paper.
2. Color the patterns and cut them out.
3. Glue the pig's head to the flat bottom of the bag.
4. Glue the mouth beneath the bottom flap.
5. Put your hand inside the bag and make the pig talk.

Finished Product

Jesus Deals with Demons

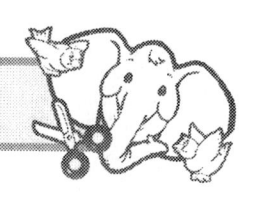

Craft: Bible Story Picture Pack

Materials

- Bible story pictures on pages 109 and 110
- box pattern on page 111
- cardstock or poster board
- scissors
- tape or glue
- crayons, markers, or colored pencils

Directions

1. Copy the box pattern onto cardstock or poster board.
2. Color the pattern and cut it out.
3. Fold the pattern on the broken lines.
4. Glue or tape the tabs to fasten the box.
5. Color the pictures on pages 109 and 110.
6. Cut apart the pictures and put them in the pack.
7. Take them out to review the story.

Finished Product

Jesus Heals a Demon-Possessed Man

Jesus met a demon-possessed man.

1

Jesus Heals a Demon-Possessed Man

The man shouted,
"What do you want with me, Jesus?"

2

Jesus Deals with Demons

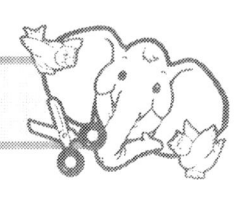

Craft: Bible Story Picture Pack *(cont.)*

Jesus Heals a Demon-Possessed Man

Jesus commanded the demons to come out of the man. They went into some pigs.

3

Jesus Heals a Demon-Possessed Man

The pigs ran into a lake and were drowned.

4

Jesus Heals a Demon-Possessed Man

The healed man sat and talked with Jesus.

5

Jesus Heals a Demon-Possessed Man

Jesus told him; go home and tell what God has done for you.

6

Jesus Deals with Demons

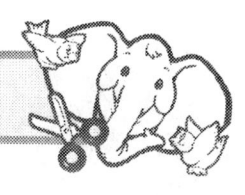

Craft: Bible Story Picture Pack *(cont.)*

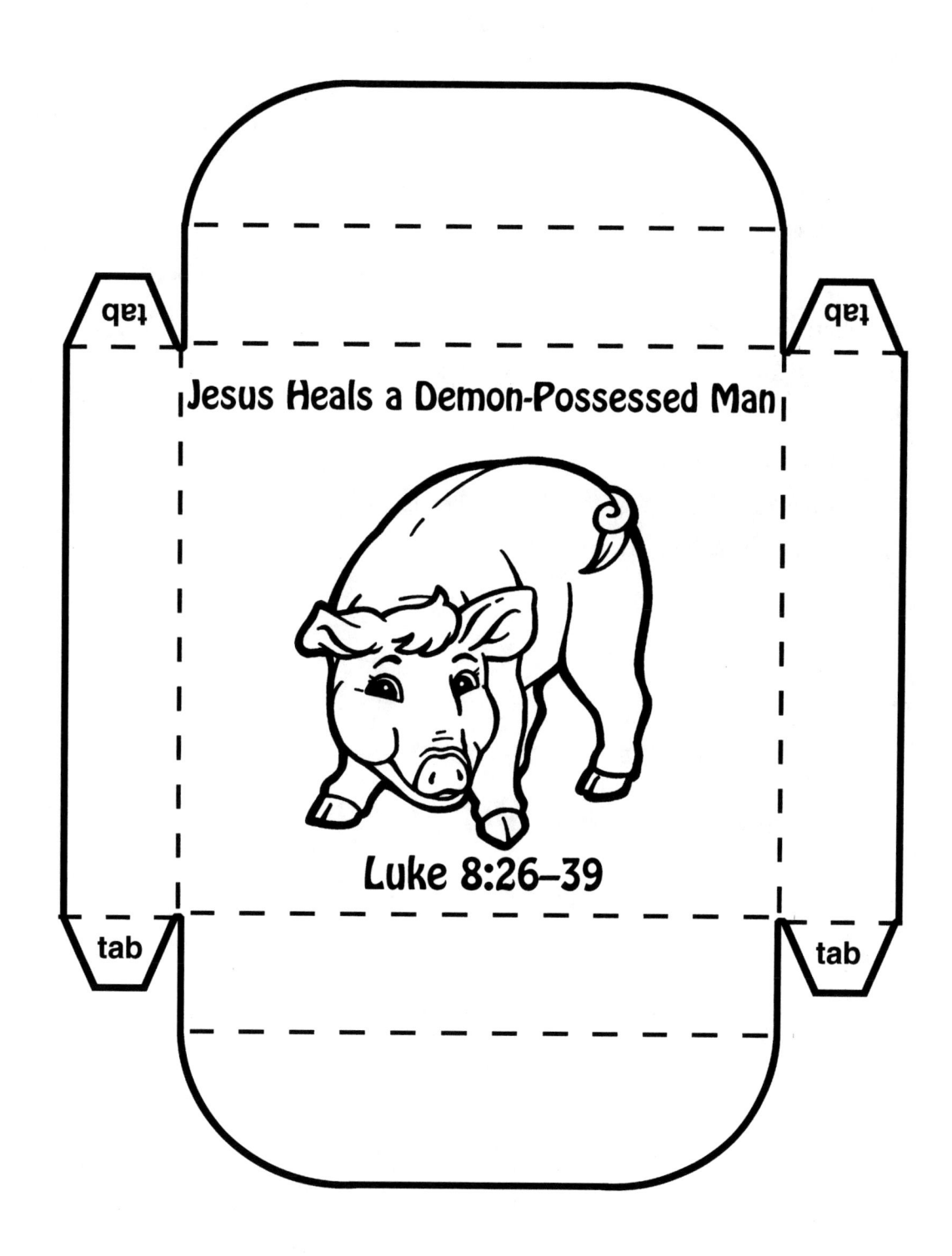

Jesus Heals a Demon-Possessed Man

Luke 8:26–39

tab tab tab tab

©*Teacher Created Resources* — 111 — #7061 *Bible Stories & Crafts: Animals*

Jesus Deals with Demons

Craft: Paper Plate Pig

Materials

- patterns on pages 112 and 113
- white paper
- crayons, markers, or colored pencils
- paper plate
- scissors
- glue or glue stick

Directions

1. Copy the patterns onto white paper.
2. Color the patterns and cut them out.
3. Color the paper plate.
4. Glue the head on the paper plate.
5. Glue the pig's feet to the bottom of the plate as shown.
6. Cut out the word strip and glue it on the plate.

Finished Product

Whatever your problem,
Jesus can fix it!
Luke 8:26–39

Jesus Deals with Demons

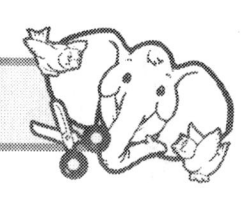

Craft: Paper Plate Pig *(cont.)*

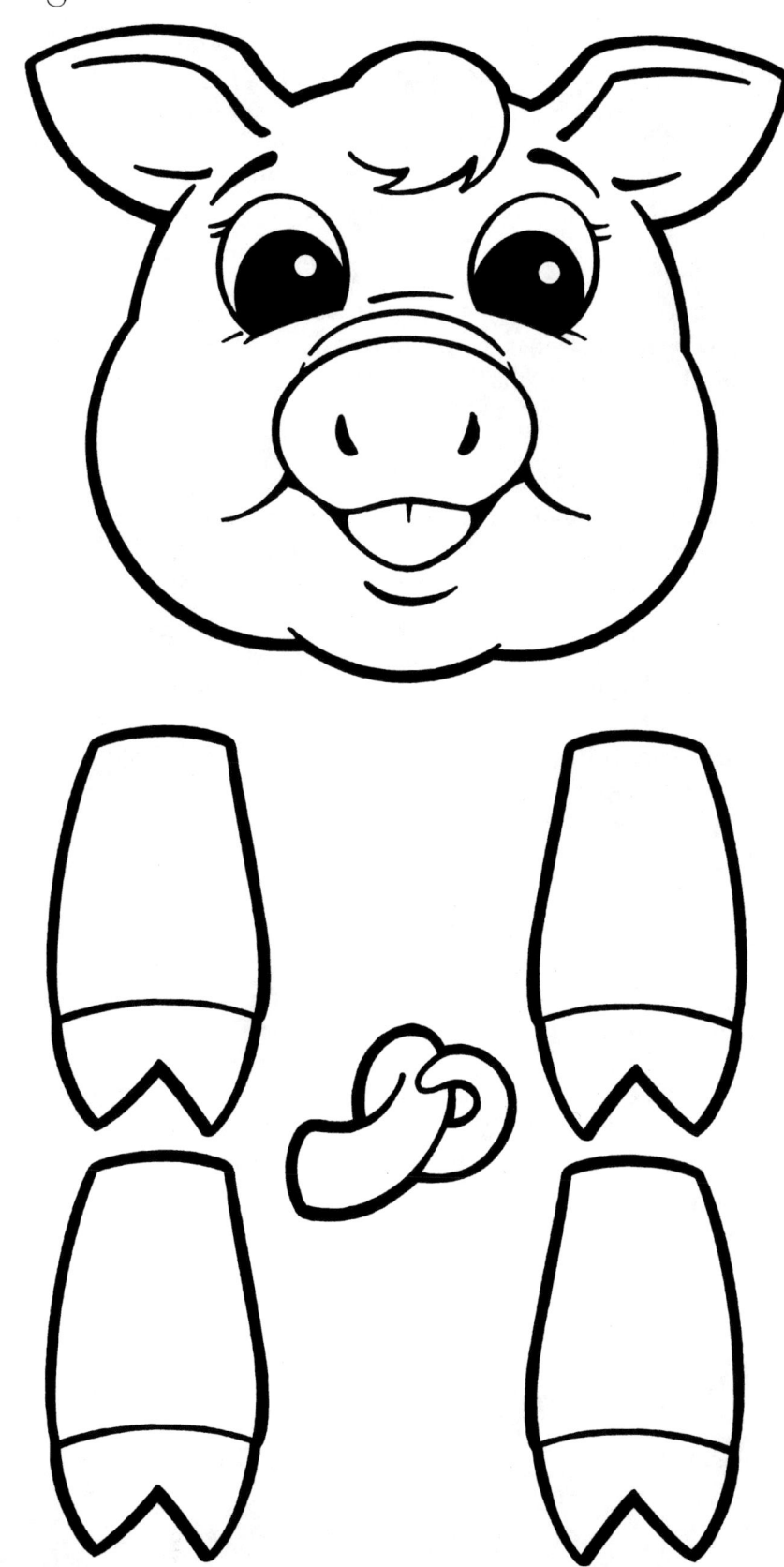

113

©Teacher Created Resources

#7061 Bible Stories & Crafts: Animals

Jesus Talks About Sparrows

Bible Story: Matthew 10:28-31

As you tell the children what Jesus said about sparrows, draw a bird on the board in four parts: body, head, wings, and feet. Draw one part of the sparrow for each point Jesus made.

Jesus chose 12 men to be His special followers called disciples. He was sending them out on their own to tell people about Him. He even gave them power to do miracles of healing. But before they left, He wanted to encourage them. So He talked to them about sparrows.

Sparrows? Why would Jesus talk to His disciples about such a common, ordinary bird? There are so many sparrows in the world, most people do not even notice them. Many people consider them a nuisance and try to keep them away from bird feeders. What in the world could Jesus teach His disciples, and us, from sparrows?

First, Jesus told His disciples not to be afraid. He reminded them that what other people could do to them amounted to a big zero! (*1. Draw a circle for the sparrow's body.*) They should be more concerned about pleasing God than pleasing people. People might be able to hurt their bodies, but they could not touch their souls.

Then Jesus reminded them that there were so many sparrows two of them could be bought for only a penny. However, even if sparrows counted for nothing with people, God cared about them. (*2. Draw a small circle on the inside of the circle for the sparrow's head. Add eyes and a triangle beak.*) In fact, Jesus said not one sparrow could fall down without God knowing it. He is even concerned about such small creatures.

Did you know that God cares so much about you? He even knows how many hairs you have have growing on your head. It is true! Jesus said so. (*3. Draw a wing on each side of the sparrow's body and a tail.*) He assured His disciples that God knew all about them and cared what happened to them.

Finally, Jesus told His disciples, "Don't be afraid; you are worth more than many sparrows." (*4. Draw the sparrow's feet at the bottom of the circle.*) God sent Jesus to die for your sins, not for sparrows! Jesus wanted to make sure that His disciples understood that God loved them and would watch over them wherever they went. The next time you see a sparrow, remember that God cares about it, but you are far more precious to Him.

Discussion

- How does God care for sparrows?
- How does God care for you?

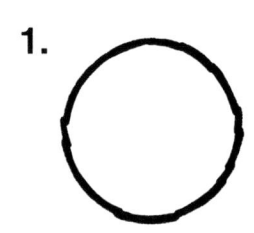

Jesus Talks About Sparrows

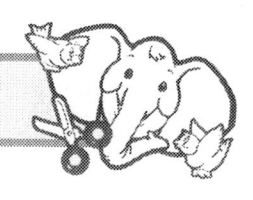

Bible Verse

"The LORD is good, a refuge in times of trouble. He cares for those who trust in him." (Nahum 1:7)

How did God show that He cares more for people than He does for sparrows?

Puppet Skit

Follow the directions on page 116 to make a sparrow head band. Let children wear their head bands as they sing and act out the following musical skit.

(*Tune:* "Mary Had a Little Lamb")

God sees all the sparrows fly

(*Pretend to fly back and forth.*)

Back and forth in the sky.

(*Keep flying.*)

And when the little sparrows fall,

(*Drop gently down to the floor.*)

God sees it and He cares.

(*Point toward heaven, then put hand over heart.*)

God sees everything I do,

(*Point to yourself.*)

And I know that it's true:

(*Shake head yes.*)

He sent His Son to die for me.

(*Stretch out arms to make your body a cross shape.*)

He sees me and He cares.

(*Point up, then put hand over heart.*)

Jesus Talks About Sparrows

Craft: Sparrow Head Band

Materials

- pattern below
- stapler and staples or tape
- crayons or colored markers
- scissors
- head strips
- cardstock

Directions

1. Copy the sparrow pattern onto cardstock.
2. Color the sparrow and cut it out.
3. Cut out the head strips. Staple or tape one strip to each side of the sparrow pattern. An extra strip is provided if two strips do not fit the head.
4. Hold the head band on your head to figure out what size you need.
5. Staple or tape the strips together and cut off the extra so the head band fits loosely around your head.

Finished Product

#7061 Bible Stories & Crafts: Animals © Teacher Created Resources

Jesus Talks About Sparrows

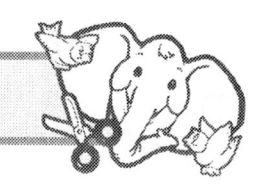

Craft: "Jesus Cares" Banner

Materials

- patterns on pages 117 and 118
- cardstock paper
- crayons, markers, or colored pencils
- scissors
- glue or glue stick
- string or yarn
- hole punch

Finished Product

Directions

1. Copy the patterns onto cardstock.
2. Color the patterns and cut them out.
3. Glue the birds on the banner.
4. Punch holes in the top of the banner and add yarn or string to hang it.

Jesus Talks About Sparrows

Craft: "Jesus Cares" Banner *(cont.)*

JESUS

Cares

For every little sparrow, and even more for you!

Jesus Talks About Sparrows

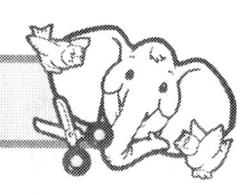

Craft: 3-D Tissue Paper Picture

Materials

- patterns on pages 119 and 120
- cardstock paper
- crayons, markers, or colored pencils
- glue
- scissors
- green tissue paper

Directions

1. Copy the patterns onto cardstock paper.
2. Color the sparrow pattern and the tree scene on page 120.
3. Cut out the sparrow and nest and glue it in place on the tree.
4. Cut green tissue paper into 1" squares.
5. Crumple the green tissue paper squares into small balls.
6. Glue the balls in bunches at the ends of the branches.

Finished Product

Jesus Talks About Sparrows

Craft: 3-D Tissue Paper Picture *(cont.)*

Glue bird nest here.

Sparrow in the tree,
God cares for you and me.
He knows each time you fall,
And He hears me when I call.

The Good Shepherd

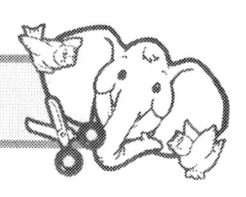

Bible Story: John 10:1-15; Psalm 23

Use some simple props to tell about the Good Shepherd. You will need something to represent a shepherd's staff, such as a cane or a long stick with a curved top, and a shorter, thick stick to represent the shepherd's rod. Also, have available a simple food snack, such as small crackers or cereal, and small cups of water for the children. Have them sit on the floor and pretend to be sheep as you act the part of the shepherd.

Everyone in Bible times knew what a shepherd did because almost everyone had sheep. The shepherd had to take care of his flock of sheep and lead them where they needed to go. David wrote a psalm all about how the Lord is our shepherd.

He said the shepherd leads the sheep to green pastures where they can have plenty to eat. (*Hand out the food treat and let children eat it.*)

The shepherd also leads the sheep to quiet water because they are easily frightened and will not drink from a running stream. (*Hand out cups of water for the children to drink.*)

He protects the sheep from wild animals, sometimes using his rod to hit the wolf or bear to drive it away. (*Pretend to hit something with the rod.*) And when a sheep is lost or in trouble, the shepherd goes to look for it. (*Have one of the children crawl under a table or go into a corner.*) When he finds it, he rescues it, sometimes by reaching down to it with his staff. (*Hold out the staff to the child to grab, then pull him out.*)

Jesus called Himself the Good Shepherd. He said He knew each one of His sheep by name. That showed how much He cared about them. He protected them and did everything He could to help them. In fact, Jesus even gave His life for His sheep.

Who were the sheep Jesus was talking about? The Bible tells us that we are like sheep. He loves and cares for us like a shepherd. Anyone who has ever raised sheep knows that they are not very smart animals. They are not able to take care of themselves because they do foolish things. That is why they need a shepherd to take care of them.

People are not very smart either. We disobey God and make foolish choices sometimes. We cannot be the people God wants us to be on our own. That is why God sent Jesus to the earth to be our Good Shepherd. And Jesus even died so we could have our sins forgiven. If we love and follow Him, we will please God and our sins will be forgiven.

Discussion

Psalm 23 tells us, "The Lord is my shepherd, I shall not be in want."

- What do you think that means?
- What do you think is the best thing your Good Shepherd has done for you?

The Good Shepherd

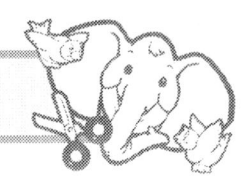

Bible Verse

"We are his people, the sheep of his pasture." (Psalm 100:3b)

How can we show our thanks to Jesus for being our Good Shepherd?

Puppet Skit

Follow the directions on page 123 to make a sheep sock puppet. Let children use their puppets to act out the puppet skit below.

Sheep 1:	Ah, what a nice morning. I think I'll go for a walk.
Sheep 2:	Hey, where are you going?
Sheep 1:	For a walk.
Sheep 2:	By yourself? Shouldn't you wait for the shepherd?
Sheep 1:	Naaa! I feel like having an adventure today. See you later.
Sheep 3:	Where is Snowflake headed?
Sheep 2:	Right for trouble I think. He shouldn't wander off by himself.
Sheep 4:	Here comes the shepherd to count us.
Sheep 5:	We are all here, aren't we? Why is he stopping?
Sheep 3:	Snowflake went off on his own.
Sheep 5:	Oh no! What a dumb thing to do. Now the shepherd will have to go find him.
Sheep 6:	What is going on? I'm hungry! Why isn't the shepherd leading us to the pasture?
Sheep 4:	We can't go anyplace right now. The shepherd is going to look for Snowflake.
All Sheep:	Baaa! Baaa! Baaa!
Later	
Sheep 3:	Here comes the shepherd, and he has Snowflake on his shoulders.
Sheep 6:	It is about time! I am starving. He should have just let Snowflake stay lost.
Sheep 2:	The shepherd would never do that. He cares about us, all of us!

The Good Shepherd

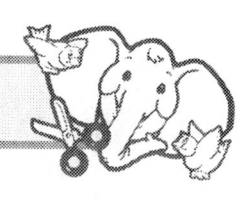

Craft: Sheep Sock Puppet

Materials

- tube sock
- cotton balls
- red marker
- scissors
- felt or fabric (pink and black)
- 3 buttons per puppet
- glue

Directions

1. Put the tube sock on your hand. Push in the center part of the sock and use your thumb and fingers to make a mouth. Use the red marker to mark the center of the mouth where you will glue the sheep's tongue.

2. Take the sock off your hand. Trace around the tongue pattern on pink felt or fabric and cut it out.

3. Glue the tongue to the sock where you put the red mark.

4. Glue two buttons on the sock above the mouth for eyes and one at the end of the sock for a nose.

5. Trace the ear pattern twice on black felt or fabric.

6. Glue the ears on the puppet's head.

7. Glue cotton balls on the sock for the sheep's wool.

8. Let the glue dry thoroughly. Then put the sock on your hand and move your thumb and fingers to make the sheep puppet talk.

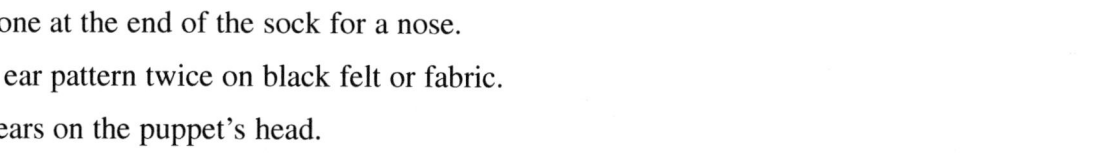

Finished Product

Tongue Pattern

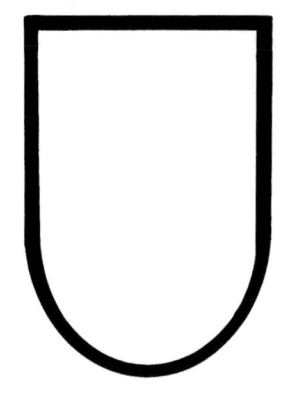

Ear Pattern

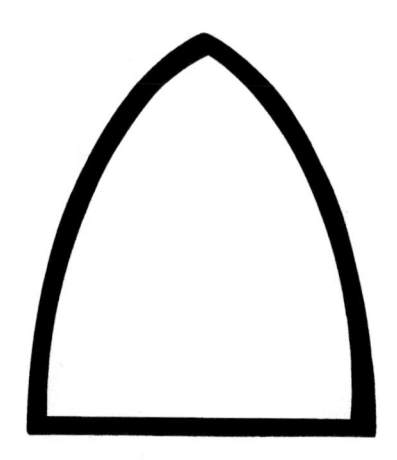

©Teacher Created Resources #7061 Bible Stories & Crafts: Animals

The Good Shepherd

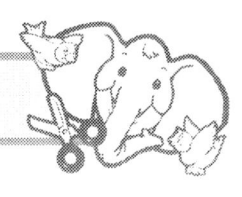

Craft: Lamb Picture Frame

Materials

- pattern on page 125
- cardstock or poster board
- scissors
- glue or tape
- photo of yourself
- paper towel or bathroom tissue tube

Directions

1. Copy the pattern onto cardstock or poster board.
2. Cut out the middle of the pattern.
3. Cut out a square of cardstock a little bigger than the cut out area on the pattern.
4. Glue or tape three sides of the square to the back of the pattern. Make sure you are able to slide a picture through one side.
5. Cut a 4" end off the paper tube.
6. Glue the end piece of the paper tube to the back of the pattern for a stand.
7. Slip your photo into the frame.

Finished Product

The Good Shepherd

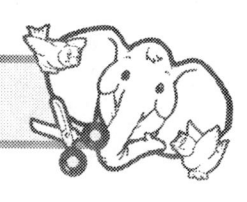

Craft: Lamb Picture Frame *(cont.)*

I am Jesus' lamb and He is my Shepherd.

Cut out.

The Good Shepherd

Craft: Torn-Paper Sheep Picture

Materials

- verse strip
- 9" x 12" construction paper (blue, dark and light green, and white)
- black marker
- scissors
- glue

Directions

1. Use blue paper for the background of your picture.
2. Tear light green paper and glue it to the bottom half of the blue paper for grass. Tear dark green paper and glue it to the middle of the picture for a hill as shown below.
3. Tear oval-shaped sheep bodies and circular heads from white paper.
4. Glue the bodies and heads onto the picture.
5. With a marker, draw legs, ears, and eyes.
6. Cut out the Bible verse strip and glue it to the top of the picture.

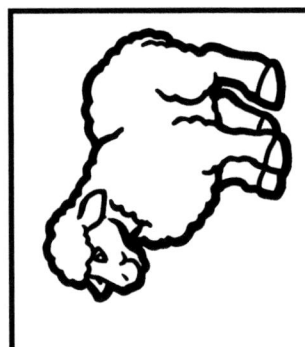

We are his people, the sheep of his pasture. (Psalm 100:3b)

Finished Product

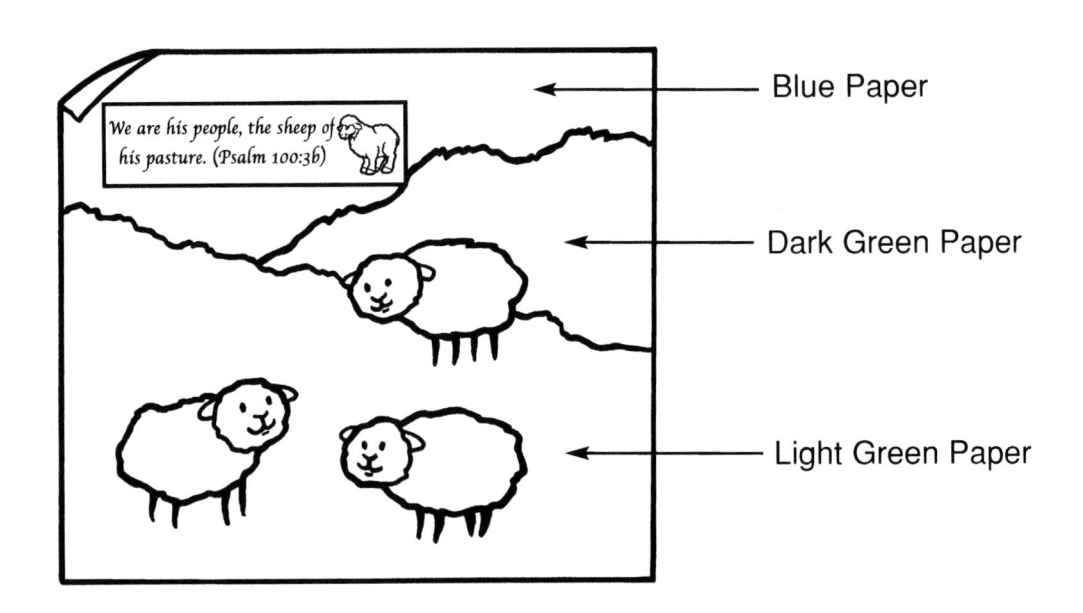

- Blue Paper
- Dark Green Paper
- Light Green Paper

Peter Pays His Taxes

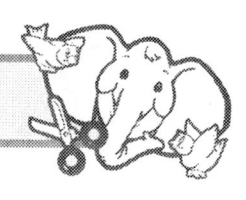

Bible Story: Matthew 17:24-27

Choose two other people who read well to act out the story skit with you.

Narrator: One day when Peter was on his way to see Jesus, the local tax collectors stopped him. They asked Peter if Jesus did not pay the temple tax. "Of course He pays it," Peter told them. Every Jewish person 20 years and older has to pay the yearly tax to help support the temple. They had not paid it yet, but Peter knew they would. Jesus believed in keeping the Law. Peter walked away and went to the house where Jesus was. Of course, as soon as Peter walked in Jesus knew what had happened, even before Peter had a chance to tell Him.

Jesus: What do you think, Simon Peter? From whom do kings collect taxes—from their own sons or from others?

Peter: From others.

Jesus: So, their own family members do not have to pay?

Narrator: Peter thought Jesus meant that since He was God's Son, He should not really have to pay the tax, and neither should His disciples.

Jesus: But we do not want to offend anyone over such a small thing, so I am sending you to get the money to pay our taxes.

Peter: Where will I get it?

Jesus: I want you to go fishing, Simon Peter. Go to the lake and throw your line into the water. Take the first fish you catch. Open its mouth and you will find a coin inside. It will be enough for you to pay our taxes.

Peter: Huh? I am to get the tax money out of a fish's mouth?

Jesus: Go, do it.

Narrator: It was the craziest thing Peter had ever heard of! But he did what Jesus told him and, sure enough, Peter found a coin in the fish's mouth, just the amount needed for the taxes. Peter took the coin and paid the tax collectors who had been giving him a hard time. Finding that coin in the fish's mouth was a miracle. Peter had seen Jesus do miracles such as healing the sick and blind, raising the dead, and calming the sea, but Peter had never seen Him do anything like this before! Peter wondered how long that fish was swimming around with that coin in its mouth. Only Jesus knows.

Discussion

- Why do you think Jesus chose such an unusual way to get money for the temple tax?
- If you had been Peter, would you have believed Jesus and obeyed Him or would you ignore such silly instructions?
- The Lord expects us to obey Him, even when we do not understand or it does not make sense. What does this story teach us about whom or what the Lord can use?

Peter Pays His Taxes

Bible Verse

"If you love me, you will obey what I command." (John 14:15)

Are there some of God's commands that don't make sense to you? What will you do about them?

Puppet Skit

Follow the directions on page 129 to make fish from pipe cleaners. Let children use their puppets to act out the action rhyme skit.

"Time to pay the temple tax," the tax collectors said.

(*Move index finger as if scolding.*)

"Jesus will pay it very soon," Peter said with a shake of his head.

(*Shake head "yes."*)

Jesus sent Peter down to the lake to do some fishing that day.

(*Pretend to throw a line into the water.*)

And in the first fish Peter caught, he found the money to pay.

(*Hold up your fish and pretend to look into its mouth.*)

Where was the money? I'll tell you where, but you just won't believe it.

(*Point to someone and shake head "no."*)

The money was in the fish's mouth, and Peter gladly retrieved it!

(*Pretend to take a coin from the fish's mouth.*)

Money in a fish's mouth? "How could it happen?" you say.

(*Hold out the fish and shrug shoulders.*)

God put the coin in that fish's mouth for Peter to find that day.

(*Point toward heaven, then toward the fish.*)

Peter Pays His Taxes

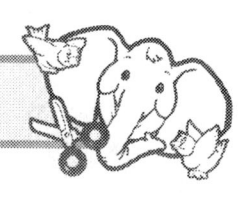

Craft: Pipe Cleaner Fish

Materials

- pipe cleaners (chenille stems)
- string *(optional)*
- pencil or ruler *(optional)*
- paper clip *(optional)*

Directions

1. Twist two pipe cleaners together at one end.
2. Twist them together at the other end too, leaving enough on the end to look like a fish tail.
3. Stretch the pipe cleaners into the shape of a fish.

(*Optional:* Tie a string to a pencil or ruler for a fishing pole. Tie a paper clip to the other end of the string for a hook. Stretch out the end of the paper clip to make it more like a curved hook. Put your pipe cleaner fish on the floor. Try to "catch" the fish by hooking it with your paper clip hook as you say the action rhyme skit on page 128.)

Finished Product

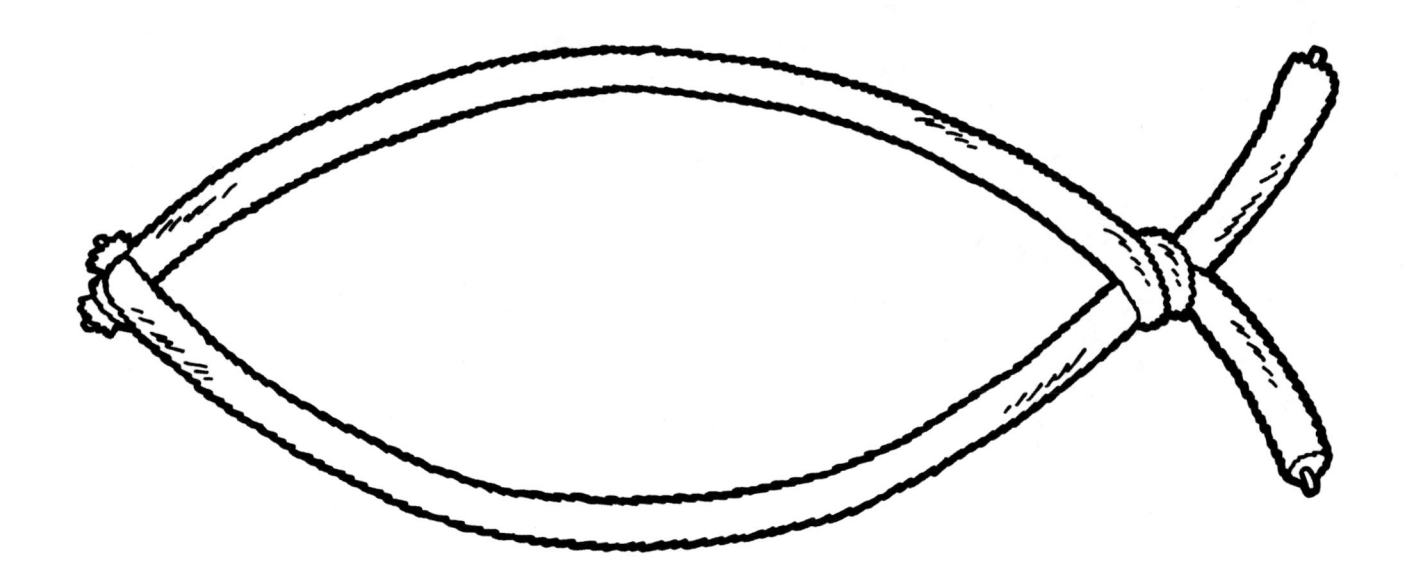

Peter Pays His Taxes

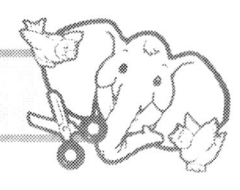

Craft: Fish Picture

Materials

- pattern on page 131
- colored yarn
- glitter or glitter glue
- cardstock or poster board
- glue

Directions

1. Copy the pattern onto cardstock or poster board.
2. Glue different colors of yarn around the fish outline.
3. Trace the letters of Jesus' name in glue, then sprinkle glitter on them.
4. Explain that this fish shape was the symbol for those who followed Jesus, such as Peter. It still stands for Christians today.

Finished Product

Peter Pays His Taxes

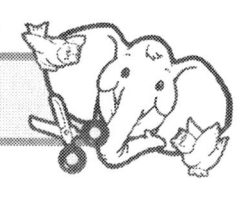

Craft: Fish Picture *(cont.)*

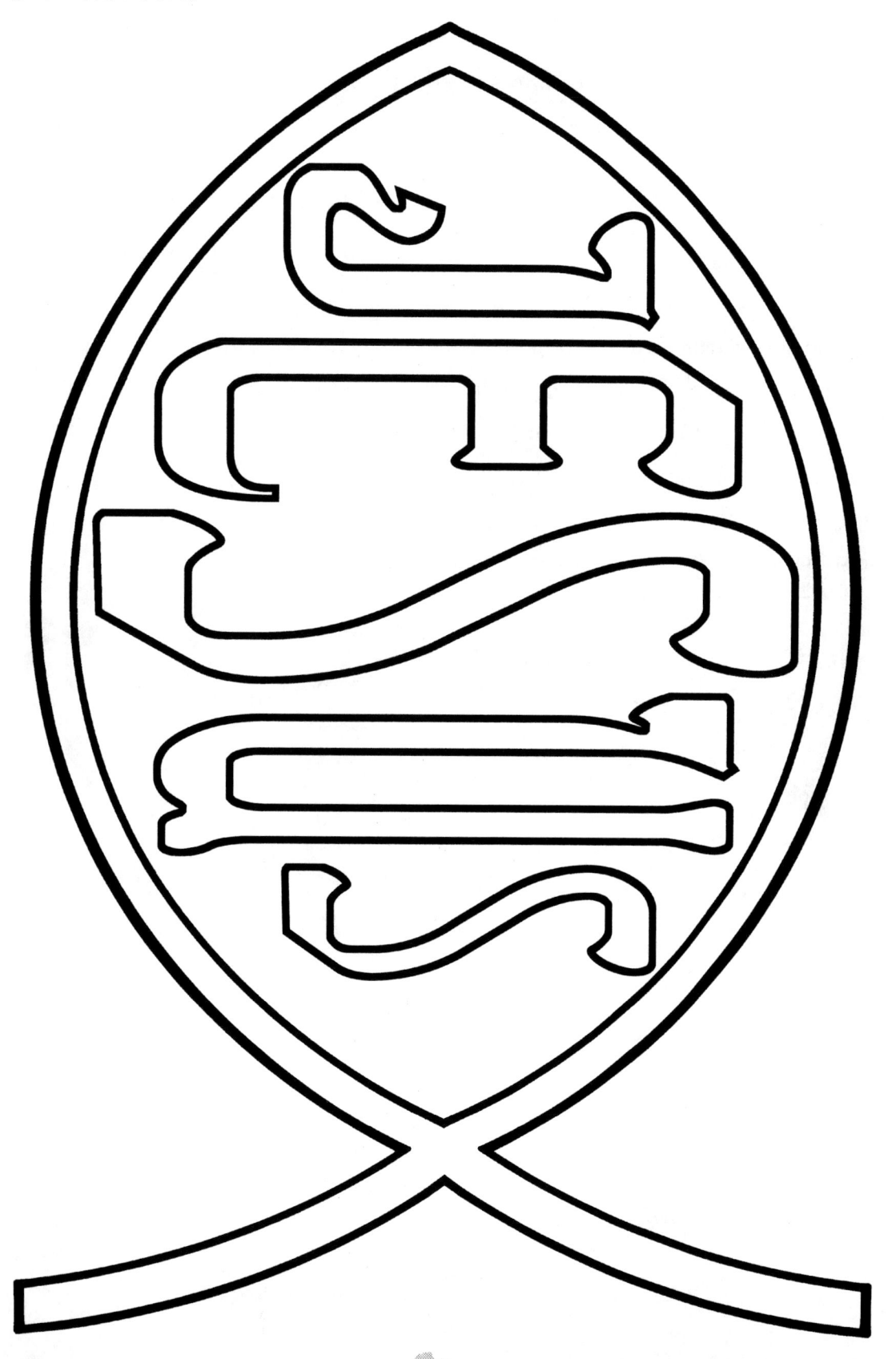

Peter Pays His Taxes

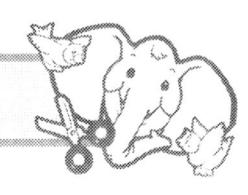

Craft: Fish Foil Art

Materials

- pattern, below
- aluminum foil
- craft eye
- glue
- hole punch
- cardstock or poster board
- sequins
- scissors
- string

Finished Product

Directions

1. Copy the pattern onto cardstock or poster board.
2. Cut out the pattern and wrap it in aluminum foil, leaving some little bumps and wrinkles.
3. Glue sequins on the foil-covered fish for scales.
4. Glue a craft eye in place.
5. Punch a hole in the top of the fish.
6. Use string to hang the fish in a window where the sun can make it sparkle.

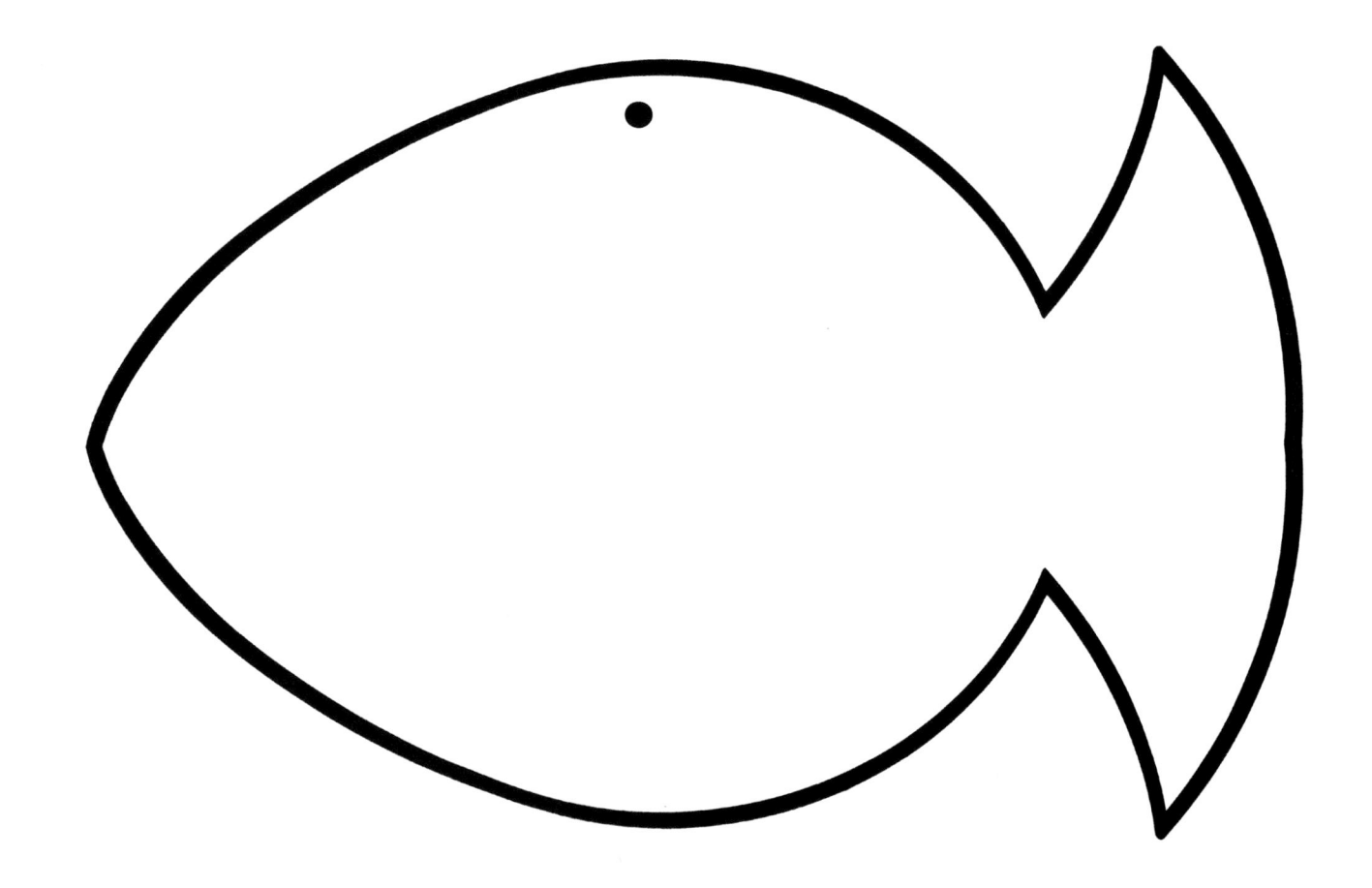

Jesus Rides into Jerusalem

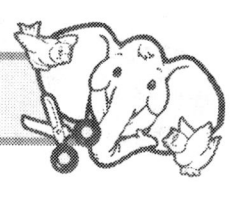

Bible Story: Luke 19:29-40

Let children help you act out this story. Provide paper palm branches for them to wave and lay down. Give some old pieces of clothing to lay down. You can pretend to be Jesus riding into town. Have the children line up on either side of you as a crowd would line up to watch a parade.

Jesus knew it was almost time for Him to die, and the city of Jerusalem was the place where it would happen. He could have stayed away, but He willingly took His disciples and headed for Jerusalem. Near the end of town, Jesus stopped and sent two of His disciples to a nearby village on an errand. He told them they would find a young donkey tied there. They were to untie it and bring it to Him. If anyone tried to stop them, they only had to say that the Lord needed it.

The disciples did exactly what Jesus told them. When they brought the donkey to Him, Jesus sat on it to ride into Jerusalem. This fulfilled an Old Testament prophecy that said God's Son would ride into town on a donkey no one else had ever ridden before. As He rode into the city, word of His arrival spread quickly and people began lining the street to see Him. (*Have children make two lines. You pretend to ride down the middle.*)

Jesus was well known and popular with the people of Jerusalem. They had heard that He could heal sick people, give sight to the blind, and even raise the dead! Many of them had seen Him perform these miracles and heard Him teach about God's love. They wanted to see Him and welcome Him to town. They broke branches off nearby palm trees and waved them in the air. "Blessed is the king who comes in the name of the Lord!" they shouted. Some of them took off their robes and threw them in the road for Jesus to ride over. (*Keep "riding" as the children wave palm branches and throw clothes in your path.*)

Back in Bible times when a famous warrior or conquering hero came into town, this was the way people welcomed him. Many people believed Jesus was God's Son and they gladly welcomed Him as a hero. But other people did not.

Some religious leaders were angry at the way Jesus was being received. They told Jesus He should make His followers stop saying such things. Jesus said to them, "If they keep quiet, the stones will cry out." Jesus meant that He was the Messiah, and if the people were not allowed to say it, God would proclaim the news some other way! The religious leaders didn't understand. They just wanted to get rid of Jesus. And before the week was up, they would do it.

Discussion

- Read Zechariah 9:9. What this Old Testament prophet said hundreds of years before Jesus was born came true. Were the other things he said in the verse true of Jesus?

- Why do you think it was so important for Jesus to fulfill prophecy? (It proved that He was the Messiah, not just someone claiming to be God's Son.)

- If Jesus came into your town today, how do you think people would receive Him? How would you receive Him?

Jesus Rides into Jerusalem

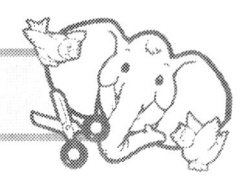

Bible Verse

"Let us rejoice and be glad in his salvation." (Isaiah 25:9b)

Why should knowing Jesus make us glad?

Puppet Skit

Follow the directions on page 135 to make donkey ear head bands. Let children wear their head bands to act out the imaginary conversation of five donkeys. Those without reading parts can make donkey noises as indicated.

Donkey 1:	It is about time you got back. Where have you been, little donkey?
Donkey 2:	You will never believe it! It was amazing! I wish you all could have been there to see it.
Donkey 3:	Been where? Seen what?
Donkey 2:	This morning my master tied me to a tree and just left me there. I did not know why. Then two men came and untied me and led me away.
Donkey 4:	Where did they take you, little donkey?
Donkey 2:	They took me to a man named Jesus.
Donkey 1:	I have heard about Him. He can do miracles!
Donkey 3:	What did Jesus want with a little donkey like you? You have never even been ridden before.
All Donkeys:	(*Donkeys "hee-haw" as if laughing and making fun.*)
Donkey 2:	Yes, but I have been ridden now. Jesus rode me into Jerusalem.
Donkey 5:	What is so great about that? We have all been to Jerusalem.
Donkey 2:	But this was like a big parade! As I took Jesus down the road, crowds of people lined the way, shouting their welcome to Him. They even threw their robes and palm branches in the road for me to walk on. I felt like a mighty war horse bringing a hero into town.
Donkey 5:	Jesus is not a war hero. I wonder why the people welcomed Him that way.
Donkey 2:	I do not know, except they kept calling Him "the king who comes in the name of the Lord."
Donkey 4:	Well, you had an exciting day, didn't you little donkey? We are all proud of you.
All Donkeys:	(*Donkeys "hee-haw," shake their heads, and stomp their feet.*)
Donkey 2:	It is a day I will always remember. I wonder if anyone else will remember it.

Jesus Rides into Jerusalem

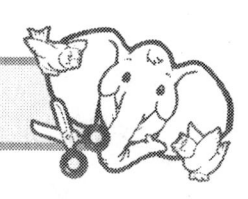

Craft: Donkey Ears Headband

Materials
- donkey ears pattern below
- cardstock
- crayons or colored markers
- head strips below
- scissors
- stapler and staples or tape

Directions
1. Copy the ears onto cardstock.
2. Color the ears and cut them out.
3. Cut out the head strips. Staple or tape one to each side of the ears.
4. Hold the head band on your head to figure out what size you need.
5. Staple or tape the strips together and cut off the extra so the head band fits loosely on your head.

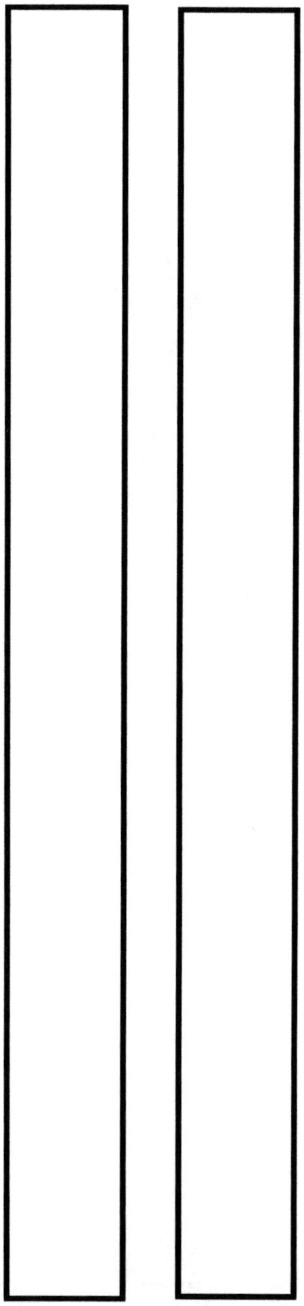

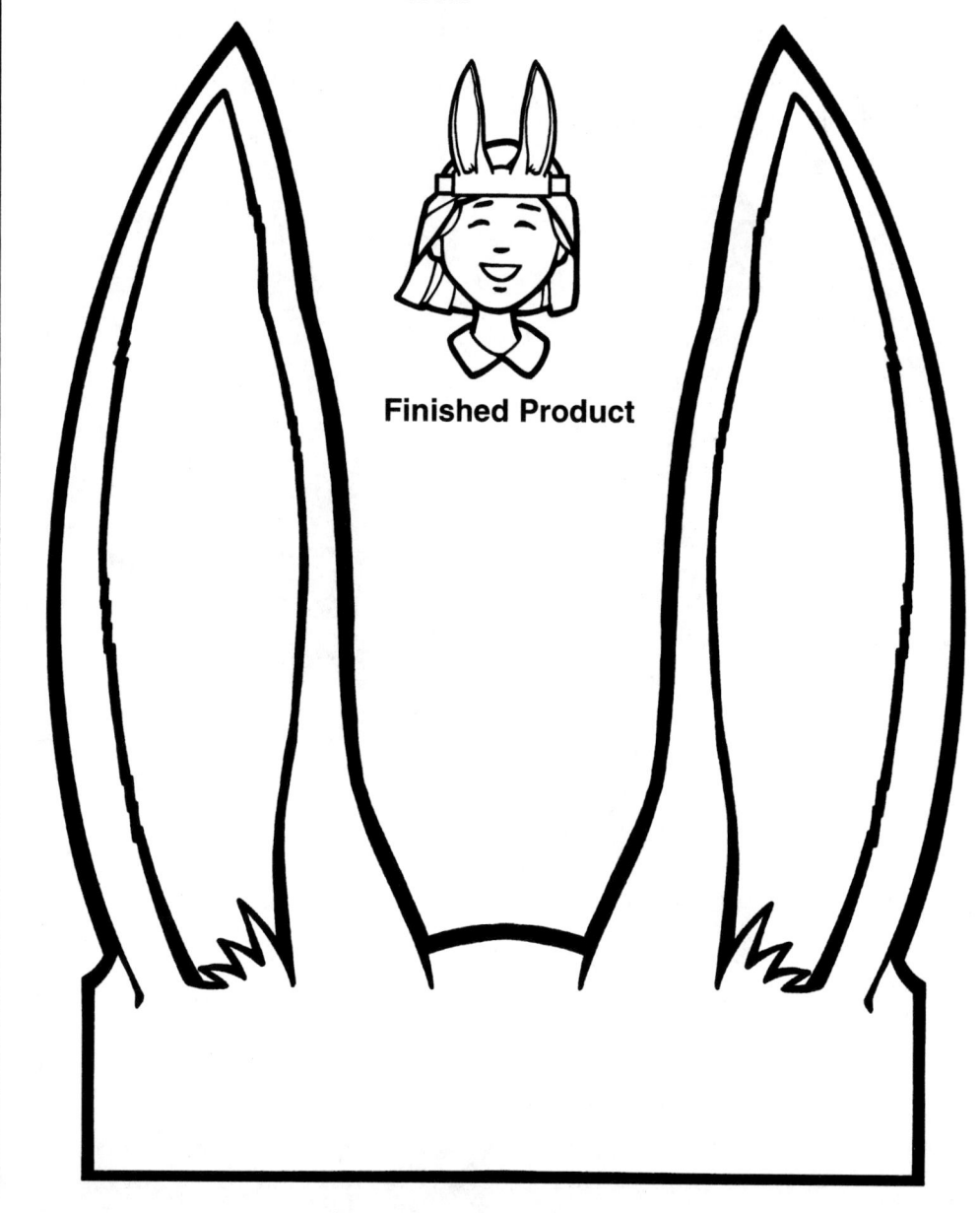

Finished Product

©Teacher Created Resources   #7061 Bible Stories & Crafts: Animals

Jesus Rides into Jerusalem

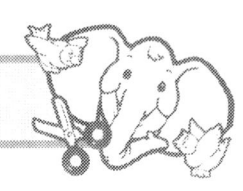

Craft: Donkey Prayer Bag

Materials

- pattern below
- brown paper lunch sack
- crayons, markers, or colored pencils
- white paper
- writing utensils
- scissors

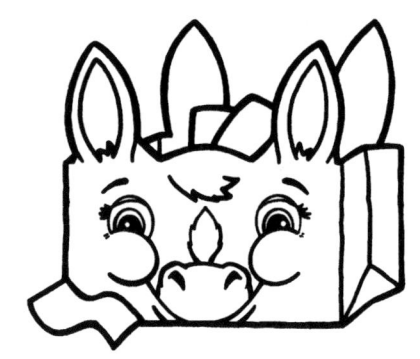

Finished Product

Directions

1. Make two copies of the donkey pattern onto white paper.
2. Color each donkey.
3. Cut out and glue the patterns to both sides of a brown paper lunch sack.
4. Cut around the ears on the bag as shown, front and back.
5. Write prayer requests and reminders on paper strips and keep them in the donkey bag. Pray for each one as you take it out.

#7061 Bible Stories & Crafts: Animals   ©Teacher Created Resources

Jesus Rides into Jerusalem

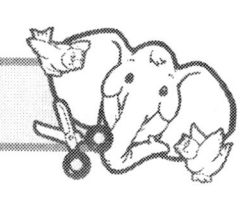

Craft: Service Card Box

Materials

- patterns and cards on pages 137 and 138
- cardstock
- scissors
- crayons, markers, or colored pencils
- glue

Finished Product

Directions

1. Copy the patterns onto cardstock.
2. Color your patterns and cut them out.
3. Fold the box pattern on the broken lines. Cut and glue the tabs to form a narrow box. Make sure the text faces the inside of the box as shown.
4. Glue the donkey to the front of the box.
5. Put the service cards in the box. Take one out every day or two to remind yourself how God wants to use you.

Be kind and compassionate to one another, forgiving each other.

(Ephesians 4:32a)

Tell how much God has done for you.

(Luke 8:39a)

©Teacher Created Resources — #7061 Bible Stories & Crafts: Animals

Jesus Rides into Jerusalem

Craft: Service Card Box *(cont.)*

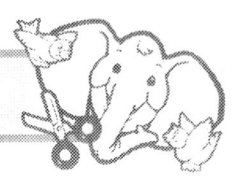

Box Pattern

Jesus chose to use a special donkey to ride into the city. He wants to use each of us in a special way. Will you let Him use you?

cut

cut

cut

cut

Serve one another in love.

(Galatians 5:13b)

Jesus said, "You did not choose me, but I chose you . . . to go and bear fruit."

(John 15:16a)

Peter Denies Jesus

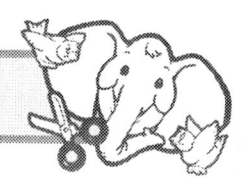

Bible Story: Mark 14:30-31, 66-72

Before you tell the Bible story, make four signs with these words on them:

1. I don't know what you're talking about!
2. I don't know Him!
3. I don't know the man you're talking about!
4. Cock-a-doodle-doo!

Give the signs to four children to hold up for everyone to read aloud when you point to each of them.

Peter had been with Jesus when He was arrested and had followed when He was taken to the high priest to be put on trial. Peter stayed in the courtyard with some other people. He could not do anything to help Jesus, but he could at least stay nearby. As Peter was warming his hands by an outdoor fire, a servant girl who worked for the high priest came by. She looked at Peter, then said, "You were with Jesus."

Earlier that evening Peter had told Jesus that he would always be true to Him and was even willing to die with Him. So what do you think Peter said when the servant girl said he had been with Jesus? (*Point to the child with the first sign to hold it up so everyone can read together "I don't know what you're talking about!"*) Though Peter was one of Jesus' best friends, he was afraid to admit it.

Peter wanted to be left alone, so he moved near the door of the courtyard. He was not there long before the servant girl told someone else, "He was one of them with Jesus." Did Peter admit to being one of Jesus' disciples this time? No, this is what he said: (*Point to the child with the second sign to hold it up so everyone can read together "I don't know Him!"*)

Peter must have been feeling uncomfortable, like everyone was watching him. After a while the people standing near him said, "Surely you are one of them, for you are a Galilean." And do you know what Peter did? He said: (*Point to the child with the third sign to hold it up so everyone can read together "I don't know the man you're talking about!"*)

The hateful words were barely out of his mouth when a rooster crowed. (*Point to the child with the fourth sign to hold it up so everyone can read together "Cock-a-doodle-doo!"*) Peter suddenly remembered how he had promised to always be faithful to Jesus and even die with Him. He also remembered clearly what Jesus had told him: "Tonight—before the rooster crows—you will disown me three times." Peter had failed the Lord and done exactly what He had said he would do. Peter broke down and cried over the horrible thing he had done.

Discussion

- Peter loved Jesus and was one of his best friends. Why do you think he denied ever knowing Him?
- Are you sometimes afraid to let people know that you love Jesus?
- Which is more important—what other people think of us or what God thinks of us?
- Do you think Jesus forgave Peter?

Peter Denies Jesus

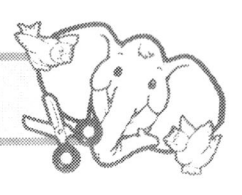

Bible Verse

"So do not be ashamed to testify about our Lord." (2 Timothy 1:8a)

Why should Christians never be ashamed to show and tell others that they love Jesus?

Puppet Skit

Follow the directions on page 141 to make a rooster stick puppet. Let children hold up their puppets and "hop" them around as they sing the song.

(*Tune:* "The Farmer in the Dell")

Cock-a-doodle-doo,

Cock-a-doodle-doo.

Listen to the message that this rooster has for you.

Cock-a-doodle-doo,

He knows what you should do.

If you love the Lord, then to Him you must be true.

Cock-a-doodle-doo,

Cock-a-doodle-doo.

Don't be like Peter who did not do what he promised to.

Cock-a-doodle-doo,

Don't be afraid, not you!

Speak up and say to everyone what Jesus means to you.

Peter Denies Jesus

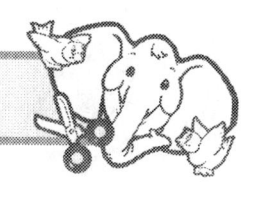

Craft: Rooster Stick Puppet

Materials

- pattern below
- scissors
- crayons or colored markers
- craft stick or tongue depressor
- cardstock
- glue or tape

Finished Product

Directions

1. Copy the rooster pattern onto cardstock.
2. Color it and cut it out.
3. Glue or tape the rooster onto a craft stick or tongue depressor for a handle.

©Teacher Created Resources · #7061 Bible Stories & Crafts: Animals

Peter Denies Jesus

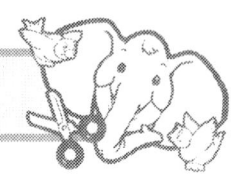

Craft: Rooster Magnet

Materials

- pattern below
- cardstock or poster board
- crayons, markers, or colored pencils
- scissors
- tape
- magnet
- assorted feathers
- glue

Finished Product

Directions

1. Copy the rooster pattern on cardstock or poster board.
2. Color the rooster and cut it out.
3. Tape feathers to the back side of the rooster.
4. Then glue a magnet on the back and place on a magnetic surface.

Cock-a-doodle-doo!
Always be true to Jesus who loves you!

#7061 Bible Stories & Crafts: Animals ©Teacher Created Resources

Peter Denies Jesus

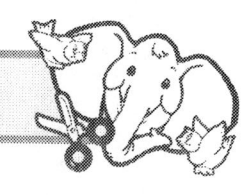

Craft: Rooster Clock

Materials

- patterns below and on page 144
- cardstock or poster board
- crayons, markers, or colored pencils
- brad fastener
- scissors
- tape or glue

Finished Product

Directions

1. Copy the patterns onto cardstock or poster board.
2. Color the patterns and cut them out.
3. Use a brad fastener to attach the hands to the clock.
4. Then tape the rooster strip to the back side of the clock as shown above.
5. Fold the stands in half.
6. Tape or glue one stand to the back of the clock and the other stand to the back of the rooster. Check to make sure the stands support the clock on a flat surface.
7. Place by your bed to remind you that "It's always time to serve Jesus."

©Teacher Created Resources   #7061 Bible Stories & Crafts: Animals

Peter Denies Jesus

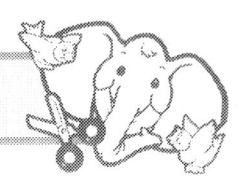

Craft: Rooster Clock *(cont.)*

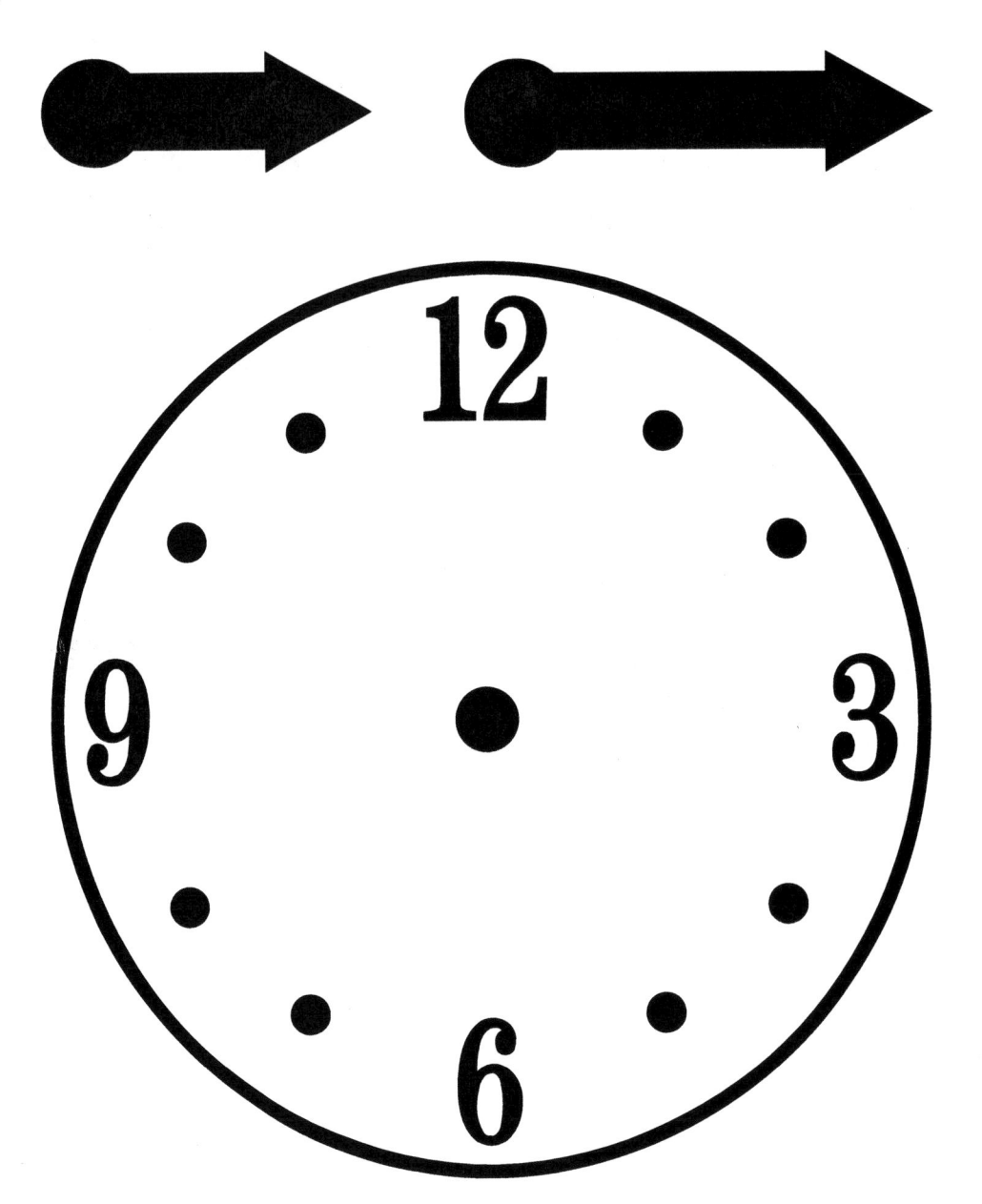

12 ... 9 ... 3 ... 6

A-Frame Patterns

Fold in half. Use to stand behind the clock.

Fold in half. Use to stand behind the rooster.

#7061 Bible Stories & Crafts: Animals ©Teacher Created Resources